Blockchain Value

Blockchain Value

Transforming Business Models, Society, and Communities

Olga V. Mack

BEP

BUSINESS EXPERT PRESS

Leader in applied, concise business books

Blockchain Value: Transforming Business Models, Society, and Communities
Copyright © Business Expert Press, LLC, 2021

First published in 2020 by
Business Expert Press, LLC
222 East 46th Street, New York, NY 10017
www.businessexpertpress.com

ISBN-13: 978-1-95253-824-7 (paperback)
ISBN-13: 978-1-95253-825-4 (e-book)

Business Expert Press Entrepreneurship and Small Business Management Collection

Collection ISSN: 1946-5653 (print)
Collection ISSN: 1946-5664 (electronic)

Cover and interior design by S4Carlisle Publishing Services Private Ltd., Chennai, India

10 9 8 7 6 5 4 3 2 1

Printed in the United States of America.

Dedication

*To my digital twins. You have always been
there for me. I wish you were mine.*

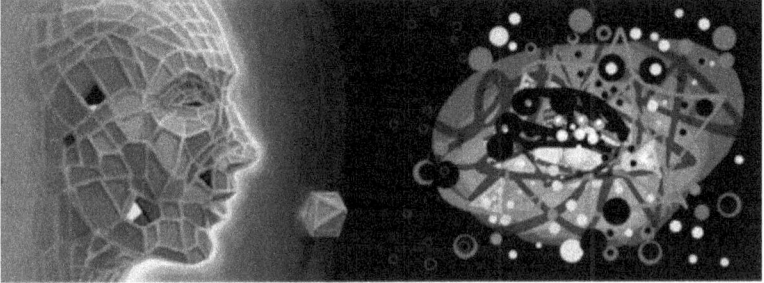

DADA Collective: Boris Z. Simunich, Peru / Andras, New Zealand,
collaboratively created using blockchain technology, a visual conversation.

Praise for Blockchain Value

"Olga V. Mack presents an essential read for those seeking to demystify the practical benefits of blockchain technology."
—Daniel Spuller, Chairman, North Carolina Blockchain Initiative and former Director, Chamber of Digital Commerce

"Olga V. Mack is a leading voice in the worlds of law, technology, and innovation. In Blockchain Value, she explains, with great insight, lucidity, and humor, one of the most powerful—and least understood—technologies transforming the world today."
—David Lat, Founding Editor, Above the Law, and Managing Director, Lateral Link

"Olga V. Mack is a world-leading strategist, nationally-recognized author, public speaker, and women's advocate. In Blockchain Value, Olga's high levels of optimism for blockchain technologies and how these will transform our lives shine through. There is amusement, expert analysis, and eye-opening futurist insights. Highly recommend"
—Robert Hanna, Entrepreneur, Founder & Managing Director, Kissoon Carr, and Host, Legally Speaking Podcast

"I approached it wearing two hats – one as CEO and Founder of a FinTech start-up and the other as a blockchain technician. In both capacities, I feel that Blockchain Value is a must-read. Olga Mack takes a complicated topic and makes it accessible."
—Maryanne Morrow, CEO and Founder, 9th Gear Technologies, Inc.

Description

Blockchain is everything you don't understand about technology, finance, and law mixed together. It is a complex technology that is still largely experimental today. It will be transformative in the future. This book focuses on the nonexclusive values of blockchain that can be used across industries. Chapter 1 explores how blockchain technology adds value to data management, security, and sharing. Chapter 2 focuses on Blockchain-as-a-Service (BaaS), a method for companies to take advantage of blockchain technology more easily and quickly. Chapter 3 discusses how blockchain technology may transform our understanding of digital goods or dGoods. Chapter 4 dives into ownership and property and how blockchain technology is changing both concepts. Chapter 5 zeroes in on how blockchain technology will change how we collaborate and how this, in turn, will radically change what is possible to accomplish together. Chapter 6 dives into trust and how blockchain technology redefines what it is and how to develop it. And, finally, Chapter 7 focuses on the transformative power of small acts and micropayments amplified by blockchain.

Keywords

blockchain; smart contract; DLT; shared ledger; distributed ledger technology; entrepreneurship; e-commerce

Contents

Foreword

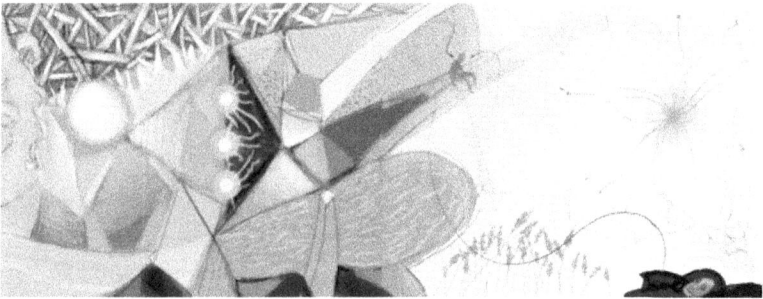

DADA Collective: Lissette San Martin, Chile / Mlibty, Croatia, collaboratively created using blockchain technology, a visual conversation

About 2 years ago, I told my husband that instead of pursuing the usual path for a thirty-something general counsel at a start-up—toward the next bigger and better company—I would dive headfirst into the blockchain business world. He was … surprised. And I am certain that, as he politely smiled and asked "why?" he was wondering if I had hit my midlife crisis earlier than expected.

"Imagine that there's a new candy store in town, with the best candies ever from all over the world," I began my explanation, watching his expression change from shock to confusion.

> Everyone is racing to the candy store, eager to get and gorge on the candy. Well, I have two choices here. I can stay general counsel and keep telling everyone how to optimize their candy enjoyment while reminding them of the various sugar-related risks, all the while secretly salivating with my hands and mouth pressed against the window of the candy store. Or I can get in and gorge on the candy. So I decided to do the latter. I'll get in early, help build the blockchain industry, and enjoy the process firsthand, instead of vicariously through the experiences of my colleagues.

He responded: "Sounds good."

When it comes to blockchain technology, I decided to get in a proverbial candy store and gorge on the candy.

And so, it happened! For the last 2 years, I have been on the front lines of this incredibly exciting and promising new industry. If you've kept up with the news at all, you might already know that the highs have been very high, and the lows have been, well, very low.

I have seen snake oil salesmen capitalize on the boom by deceiving the general public and obfuscating the technology. And I have seen the industry professionalize and filter out the phonies. I have met many so-called experts who ooze confidence but lack competence, but I have seen an increasing number of high-integrity professionals learn together and persistently develop use cases for this very complicated technology.

It is an experimental field. Doing is the only way to gain expertise.

The word "blockchain" has become a catnip for investors. At first, they were giving five, ten, twenty million dollars to any early-stage company, with no product and hardly anything to show beyond an idea—just an allegedly "amazing team" and the word "blockchain" thrown in there somewhere.

I talked to a few investors as I considered joining a few of these mysterious start-ups. I wanted to know what I was missing, what they were seeing that I wasn't. I watched highly successful, grown men behave like my 8-year-old daughters do in Claire's when they are overwhelmed by shiny objects. Thankfully, this unsustainable enthusiasm ended. We're back to a much more prudent approach to investing.

I have seen companies use "blockchain" as a marketing tool to signal novelty and innovation. And I have increasingly seen companies put a serious effort into developing the technology and ecosystem. I have had many conversations about what is possible. And I have even seen several pilots and proof of concepts enter production and materialize in the real world.

Interestingly, blockchain is not geographically limited to Silicon Valley. It is a global phenomenon. Switzerland, Estonia, and Israel are often leading the developments in this field.

Enterprises and start-ups are finally building products that are meaningful on blockchain. We are finally solving problems and building what our customers may need.

Finally, I have witnessed highly regarded professionals debate, in full seriousness, whether Hyperledger, Ethereum, or some other blockchain platform is the best. Even ignoring the seeming convergence of platforms, this debate is a bit like asking whether a fork or a spoon is a better tool. The answer is obvious: it depends on what you're eating. And sometimes chopsticks enhance the experience even more.

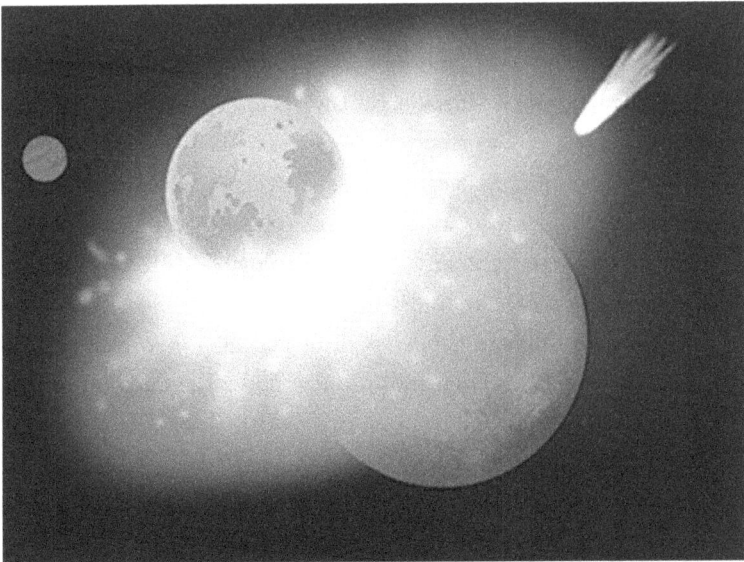

Blockchain will help beautiful and functional worlds unite into one bright, promising future.

And, yes, blockchain, just like any other technology, can be misused or at least used for unintended purposes or can have unintended consequences.

Yet I remain highly optimistic about blockchain technologies and their potential. I am convinced that blockchain technologies will transform our lives in our lifetime. The changes will grow but at first will be small and focused on efficiencies—bigger, stronger, better, faster, and cheaper.

Eventually, when we finally understand the full potential of this tool, other technologies mature, and the regulatory dust settles, we will focus on building a more functional, beautiful, and just world. Remember in the Disney film *The Little Mermaid* when Ariel uses the fork to brush her hair? She explores the potential of the tool before she can optimize its use. Once we discover the proper use of this tool called blockchain, we will start solving problems that have historically seemed unsolvable. Right now, we're still brushing our hair with a fork.

This will, of course, lead to broad innovation in business models. I remember when I started practicing law, everyone was looking for "SaaS lawyers." To be clear, "SaaS lawyers" is not a thing, at least not anymore! SaaS (software as a service) was an innovation caused by the emergence of new technology at the time. Most people didn't know much about it, so everybody was looking for SaaS lawyers to draft SaaS agreements.

Of course, in the short term, nobody could find an experienced SaaS lawyer. We had to train a generation of lawyers to negotiate and draft SaaS agreements. I am happy to report that most technology attorneys are well trained and proficient in SaaS agreements. These days "SaaS lawyers" are no longer a hot commodity; they are everywhere technology companies operate.

There's a lesson to learn here. New technology leads to new business models, which, in turn, lead to demand for new skills.

That's what I expect to happen with blockchain—new technologies, new business models, and demands for new skills. The question of business models can be broken down into two distinct questions.

The first question is what new value is created? Through research and numerous interviews, I identify seven prominent values that seem to be developing using blockchain technologies. The seven values are not exhaustive even today. They are merely those that I deem to be most promising. I expect that other values will develop over time.

The second question is, who, if anybody, can monetize this value? In this book, I primarily focus on the first question. You may think that it is premature to answer the second question, especially because the answer to the first question is still developing. Throughout the book I point out opportunities for enterprises and start-ups, though how we monetize blockchain technology will evolve in the next 5 to 10 years. So, keep an open mind and stay tuned!

New technologies and industries, like children, need time to mature. They start out reckless, at times irresponsible, and often confused—but full of potential. After all, the naïve investors throwing millions of dollars at a product they know nothing about and the snake oil salesmen deceiving them all see *something* in blockchain. It's a highly exciting, though admittedly imperfect, emerging industry, but I strongly believe that as it matures, it will be harnessed to solve problems that we haven't ever even tried to solve, problems we didn't think could be solved. It will just require discipline, creative thinking, and persistence on the part of those developing it.

Introduction

DADA Collective: Lissette San Martin, Chile / Mlibty, Croatia, collaboratively created using blockchain technology, a visual conversation

"Blockchain is everything you don't understand about technology, finance, and law mixed together," I often joke. It is a complex technology that is still largely experimental. Many projects and work that use blockchain are either in their early stages or are being done in universities.

Blockchain is no pixie dust.

In fact, Gartner categorizes many blockchain efforts as "embryonic." Yes, embryonic! So if you are wondering whether you are late to this blockchain party, the answer is no. In fact, you're just in time.

What Is Blockchain?

Blocks and chains bring some interesting images to my imagination.

What is blockchain?[1] It's a type of distributed ledger technology—one of many. At a very high level, blockchain is a time-stamped distributed, cryptographically secure database. It allows network participants to establish a trusted and immutable record of transactional data. No intermediaries are needed. It is managed by a network of computers, which is spread across various sites and not owned by any single entity.

Each of these blocks of data ("block") is secured and bound to the others using cryptographic principles ("chain"). The link between each block is called a "hash," which also serves a unique ID through cryptographic algorithm.

[1]ConsenSysn. 2019. "Answers to the 40 Most Asked Questions about Blockchain." https://media.consensys.net/answers-to-the-40-most-asked-questions-about-blockchain-2b69d1191801.

Traditional databases have a centralized client-server architecture where an authority controls the central server. This design means that there is a single point of failure when it comes to data security, alteration, and deletion. The decentralized architecture of blockchain databases addresses the weaknesses of centralized database.

Cryptology, or the highly technical art of keeping secrets, is the secret ingredient that makes it all work.

This technology is no joke. It is a lot of math! I like to think of it as a big public spreadsheet in which information is collected through a network, recorded in chronological order, and sits on top of the Internet. Cryptology, or the highly technical art of keeping secrets, is the secret ingredient that makes it all work.

Once an agreement ("consensus") is reached between these computers to store something on a blockchain, it cannot be disputed, removed, or altered without knowledge and permission. So these blocks are tamperproof.

Blockchain applications are just like conventional software applications, except they implement a decentralized architecture and crypto economic systems, which are used to increase security, foster trust, tokenize assets, and design new network incentives.

Furthermore, blockchain as a field is composed of numerous block-chains. Thus, it is more appropriate to say "blockchains" (plural) when referring to the entire field.

Blockchain technology has numerous benefits. Trusted data coordination, attack resistance, shared IT infrastructure, tokenization, and built-in incentivization are commonly cited.

Blockchains began as an open-source, public effort. Soon after, corporations developed private blockchains to manage sensitive transaction data. Many industry experts anticipate that private and public block-chains will converge.[2]

This is by no means a comprehensive explanation of blockchain. But allow me to spare you the details—I know from personal experience that when I start talking about blocks, ledgers, cryptology, and consensus, listeners' eyes start to glaze over. While I can take it personally and wonder why technical explanations of five abstract concepts one after another don't make people jump with joy, the better question is, why do people need to know exactly how blockchain works?

Think about it. Very few of us can describe how electrons are made, how they travel through wires, and how they get into our walls. Most of us treat electricity as if it were a form of magic—we press a button and the room lights up. Our inability to understand the science of electricity doesn't stop us from enjoying the benefits of electricity—a well-lit room, a warm meal, or dry hair.

Similarly, when we are in an airplane thousands of feet above the ground, we don't typically stop and ask ourselves, "How does the aerodynamics of this airplane work, and do I trust it enough to get in to the airplane and let it take me from one point to another?" In fact, I willingly spend hours watching movies suspended in the air blissfully ignorant of aerodynamics for an opportunity to visit Italy. Why? The opportunity to see the Colosseum and eat authentic pizza is enough of a benefit for me!

In other words, applications are what we generally care about, more than the details of function.

---

[2] F. Khan. 2018. "Signals in the Noise: Simplifying Ethereum for Enterprises." https://media.consensys.net/signals-in-the-noise-simplifying-ethereum-for-enterprises-dd8cdfa5729f.

So yes, we can talk about the glorious blockchain details. I find them fascinating. But it's a better use of your time, reader, to jump right into applications that illustrate why and how blockchain technology is a critical technology of our generation.

You'll see that blockchain has endless applications. It can be used to enhance social networks, messengers, games, exchanges, storage platforms, voting systems, prediction markets, online shops, and much more. This book will illustrate just some of the many ways blockchain can be used to solve previously unthinkable challenges.

Bitcoin, the First Blockchain Application, and Where It All Began

The most famous application of blockchain technology is the one for which it was originally designed: Bitcoin, a novel peer-to-peer currency. In fact, the two are so intertwined that much of the general public thinks that Bitcoin and blockchain are synonymous with cryptocurrency and blockchains. That is, of course, not true. Bitcoin is an application of blockchain technology, but it's just one.

At first, Bitcoin had no value. But over time, more and more people started to use it and it quickly picked up value. Before long, it effectively became a transparent and secure bank vault. What is the secret to its security? Bitcoin secures money in plain sight. Everyone can see the accounts, but nobody has access to it except for those who have a private key, such as Satoshi. Even more interestingly, no bank or government owns unclaimed Bitcoin.

Misconceptions surrounding Bitcoin are wide and deep. There are primarily three reasons.

One, Bitcoin is rooted in a new and somewhat crazy idea of "mining," a word that most of us associate with historic events like the California Gold Rush and coal mines of the early 20th century. Perhaps the only reason I can look beyond these historic associations is that I am the daughter of a mining engineer (the traditional, non-Bitcoin kind!), and I grew up using this word in many contexts. Solving a computational problem that allows for the formation of a chain of blocks of transactions, or "Bitcoin mining," by specialized computers is the backbone of the Bitcoin network. Miners secure and confirm Bitcoin transactions. Otherwise, the network would be vulnerable and dysfunctional. In return, miners receive newly created Bitcoins and transaction fees.

Two, Bitcoin is veiled in mystery, and lots of it! It is the brainchild of someone named Satoshi Nakamoto, a mysterious person or persons whose identity folks have been debating for years. Satoshi wrote a "Bitcoin White Paper" that proposed to make money as easy to send as sending an e-mail.

Three, the initial and most prominent uses of Bitcoin have been associated with shady, illegal transactions and vices. Its use in gambling, drug transactions, and the like have tarnished its reputation. These highly publicized illicit uses have created negative associations that are repugnant to an average person.

Yet if we can look beyond the bizarre, mysterious, and illicit (and, yes, I know it is a big "if"!), the underlying technology and its capabilities are very interesting.

Bitcoin has demonstrated the inherent effects of blockchain technology. Just like with the Internet, at the center of the blockchain are people. The more people are on a blockchain, the more valuable it becomes.

Bitcoin created a new stock market. It is open source. This means that anybody can create their own copy of it. In the process, thousands of people have created currencies. They are called "alt coins," alternatives to Bitcoin, or "cryptocurrencies," "crypto" for short. They are traded globally around the clock on new digital exchanges. That is where you see the investment and innovation happening in the last few years.

Finally, Bitcoin demonstrated that blockchain technology has numerous known benefits and may transform numerous industries. Its transparency, integrity, traceability, immutability, security, lack of need for an intermediary, and potential for a customer-focused orientation are some of the reasons why businesses are exploring and innovating with blockchain. And given the experimental nature of this technology, many of the benefits haven't been discovered yet.

And, yes, we still don't know the identity of Satoshi Nakamoto. The suspense is too much!

Blockchain, So What?!

Blockchain technology may radically change how we manage transactions, financial or otherwise, and may fundamentally transform our lives, in much the same way the Internet has. Blockchain applications are already being developed in nearly every area of life you can think of—banking, payments, security technology, forecasting, real estate, health care, logistics, transportation, and numerous others.

Back-End Tech with Many Benefits

Unlike other technologies, blockchain is inherently back-end. In this sense, it's not that different from electricity. Electricity powers factories, schools, and homes. You can put it anywhere, but you cannot physically touch it (at least not safely). In fact, blockchain, like electricity, does its job best when it's entirely invisible. The less you think about it, the better it works. And like electricity, whether blockchain succeeds, fails, or becomes a niche technology will depend on whether we can find compelling applications of this powerful technology.

Public (Permission-less) versus Permission-ed Debate

On "public blockchains" type of blockchain network, anyone can use Bitcoin's cryptographic keys, act as a node, join the network, become a miner to service the network, or seek a reward. In sum, anyone can read the chain, make legitimate changes, and write a new block into the chain. Bitcoin and Ethereum are well-known examples of public blockchains.

Bitcoin and Ethereum share many cryptographic functions, and both blockchain networks currently use a proof of work consensus algorithm. Smart contracts are the key element that distinguishes Ethereum from Bitcoin. There are other technical differences.

Blockchains can be built to require permission to read the information they contain. Of course, this limits the number of parties who can transact on the blockchain or serve the network by writing new blocks into the chain. A blockchain developer may choose to make the system of record available for everyone to read but not change. They may not wish to allow anyone to be a node, serving the network's security, transaction verification, or mining function. This is what is known as "permissioned blockchain." Hyperledger Fabric is a well-known example of a permissioned blockchain.

Permissioned blockchains may or may not involve "proof of work" or some other system requirement from the nodes.

Decentralization

Decentralization is another abstract concept that is often mentioned when blockchain is discussed but that makes normal folks' eyes glaze over. In short, it is the process of distributing and dispersing power away from a central authority, which has been the norm in recent human history.

Most institutions and organizations today are centralized. They have a single highest authority that manages them. Many platforms—Facebook, Uber, Airbnb, and numerous others—are intermediaries that operate a decentralized model of value creation. For example, Uber operates a decentralized exchange of a taxi market. The supply side of the taxi market used to be controlled by the taxi industry; Uber decentralized the supply of taxi drivers and has become an intermediary.

Bitcoin, a decentralized system, doesn't have an authority. As a result, it also does not have a single point of failure. So it is more resilient, efficient, and democratic. This feature is exactly why Bitcoin and many other blockchains and cryptocurrencies use blockchain technology.

Decentralization does not have to be binary. In fact, it exists on a spectrum. There are numerous obstacles to complete decentralization. Many blockchain companies decentralize and disintermediate where possible, but some instances will take time.

Smart Contracts, Another Application

Let's talk about another confusing sounding blockchain concept—smart contracts. These are neither smart nor contracts, at least not in the traditional sense of either word. They are most definitely not as "smart" as the professionals I interviewed for the book. And they are most definitely not

A smart contract is not unlike a very sophisticated and secure vending machine.

"contracts" that have clauses and a place to sign your name at the bottom.[3] Though there is a small overlap between smart and traditional legal contracts—that is, some legal contracts could be automated using smart contracts—this overlap is very small today.

A smart contract is a code intended to store, verify, or self-execute rules. They allow you to perform transactions automatically and without third parties. These transactions are, like contracts, written in proverbial stone, trackable, permanent, and irreversible.

A smart contract is not unlike a very sophisticated and secure vending machine. It functions based on a straightforward rule: if you insert a dollar, you get a snack. Like a vending machine, it first verifies that you have inserted the correct amount. Then it executes automatically by dispensing your snack.

Ethereum is probably the most popular smart contract platform, though there are other platforms that allow you to perform similar

---

[3]D.B. Black. 2019. "Blockchain Smart Contracts Aren't Smart and Aren't Contracts." https://www.forbes.com/sites/davidblack/2019/02/04/blockchain-smart-contracts-arent-smart-and-arent-contracts/#601f8b741e6a.

functions. For example, Hyperledger Sawtooth, an open-source enterprise blockchain platform, allows users to create secure ways to handle smart contracts, with stricter rules and consensus requirements.

Let me illustrate exactly what is possible with smart contracts. Suppose I rent an apartment. I will be required to return the landlord's digital entry key by a specified date. If the key doesn't arrive on time, the smart contract will automatically release my deposit. If I send the key before the due date, then I automatically get my deposit back. This example illustrates the if-then premise that underlies smart contracts.

This if-then premise also underlies how the entire business world operates and explains why the use of smart contracts is one of the most interesting and widely adopted applications of blockchain technology. Imagine how smart contracts can improve a supply chain composed of numerous long links that take a long time to complete. For example, smart contracts can automate, ensure transparency, increase efficiency, streamline processes, and protect from fraud at various stages of shipment tracking.

Oracles

Remember oracles in high school ancient Greece history class? (Who would have thought that, as an adult, you would be reading about miners and oracles in one chapter?!). An oracle was a priest or a priestess through whom the gods would allegedly speak. People turned to oracles for information when they didn't have enough on their own to make decisions.

Blockchain oracles function similarly. Blockchains do not have ready access to outside information and rely on oracles to supply external data—stock prices, weather information, the price of a commodity, and so on—to trigger smart contracts to execute when the terms of the contract are met. These oracles are the only connection between the blockchain and the outside world. In fact, without access to these sources of outside data, use cases for smart contracts would be minimal and insignificant.

Imaginary Money

Now, let's talk about money! It's everyone's favorite subject. You may or may not have a relationship with your kids, spouse, or parents, but you have a relationship with money. It's one of the many reasons why crypto-currency discussions trigger strong reactions and opinions from everyone involved.

Coins versus Tokens

The words "coin" and "token" are often used synonymously. That is incorrect.

Coins, altcoins, or alternative cryptocurrency coins all refer to a form of digital money, created using encryption techniques that store value over time. It is a digital equivalent of money. Bitcoin is the most famous example. Some coins are based on Bitcoin's original protocol, such as Litecoin[4] and Namecoin.[5] Other coins operate on other blockchains, such as Ripple[6] and Monero.[7] Just like money, they are fungible, divisible, acceptable, portable, durable, and have limited supply. Coins are open to the public and may be sent, received, or mined. They are not meant to perform any functions beyond acting as money.

A token is simply a quantified unit of value. Not necessarily monetary value. Like money, they are generic and can be used to define any form of value. They are also fungible and can be exchangeable between different specific types of value. Yet, unlike traditional money, tokens are much more generic. They can define a broader set of values, social capital, natu-ral capital, or cultural capital. You can receive a token of appreciation or a token of appreciation—but neither will be worth much if you take it to a bank. Also, when it comes to tokens, there is no authority or central bank. Instead, anyone can provide the service via open protocols.

In sum, like coins, tokens can be used as money inside a project's limited ecosystem. Unlike coins, however, a token gives the holder a right to participate in the network. Initially, most tokens were based on the ERC20 protocol by Ethereum. They are not mined by their owners. Nor are they primarily meant to be traded. They are sold for fiat—money that the government issues and that has no intrinsic value—or cryptocurrency

---

[4]More information about Litecoin is available at https://litecoin.org/.

[5]More information about Namecoin is available at https://namecoin.org/.

[6]More information about Ripple is available at https://ripple.com/.

[7]More information about Monero is available at http://monero.org/.

to fund the start-up's tech project, the process called initial coin offering, or ICO.

Each blockchain platform or application has its own token economy, or the design and implementation of economic systems based on blockchain technology. Just like every subway or metro system in the world has a token system, every blockchain platform or application relies on specific tokens to operate. Blockchain platform creators must use economic design principles if they want to build platforms that deliver value to their users.

A well-designed token must be exchangeable between different specific forms of value. The design must support the incentive, market, and transaction design of the platform. It must also support the needs of those who use it for traditional currency purposes. Your token must fulfill platform requirements. It must also verify that token values will sufficiently compensate any platform participants, especially if they receive tokens.

Anything can be tokenized. You can tokenize a publicly traded company by dividing it into pieces and recording the ownership on blockchain. This makes company ownership more transparent. Other things can be tokenized, too. For example, real estate can be tokenized: you can split an apartment building into component shares and then buy, sell, and trade those tokens on digital exchanges. Numerous other things, from music bands to artistic works, can be tokenized.

Stablecoins

Have you been following the prices of Bitcoin? First it was low, then it went way, way up, and then it plummeted. In between, there were many other fluctuations. This understandably makes people uncomfortable. Stablecoins were invented to address this challenge. They are cryptocurrencies designed to minimize the fluctuation of the price of the stablecoin, relative to some "stable" asset or basket of assets such as a cryptocurrency, fiat money, or exchange-traded commodities like precious metals or industrial metals.

New Ways to Raise Money: ICOs STOs, IEOs, and IDOs

A founder of a project may issue and then sell tokens at the early stage of a project to finance its start. If you buy tokens, you become part investors in the project and can use the platform. You may also use these tokens to make exchanges within the market. This way, you can get paid if you create value on the platform. In other words, you have a share of ownership over the project.

You can also hold on to your tokens. The value may appreciate as networks grow over time. As the project grows, the tokens can take on greater value for their holders. People are incentivized to join networks early to gain the benefits of the increase in token value. It also provides an alternative to raising money. Companies no longer have to offer ownership shares of their company in exchange for money; instead, they can simply sell tokens to raise initial capital for the project in what is called an ICO. The founders can monetize their networks directly by merely holding their tokens and make the network useful.

Although there were some ICO activities in 2019, they might soon be extinct. When they really picked up at the end of 2017, they raised considerably regulatory scrutiny, especially in the United States. Eventually, this led to a sharp decline in ICOs, especially amid the hype around security token offerings (STOs) and then the initial exchange offerings (IEOs).

STOs were supposed to be the next generation of ICOs. But the unrealistic and high requirements to participate got in the way, and STOs never did live up to predictions. Now, investors must be considered accredited by the U.S. Securities and Exchange Commission (SEC) to participate in STOs.

Triggered by the Binance crypto exchange launching an offering for BitTorrent in January, numerous projects going to exchanges are electing to offer the same service. This is known as an IEO. It is orchestrated by a crypto exchange on behalf of a start-up that is seeking to raise funds. In return, the start-ups pay listing fees and a percentage of the tokens sold in the IEO.

An initial DEX offering (IDO) is like an IEO, except that they are conducted on decentralized exchanges (DEX), whereas IEOs are conducted on centralized ones. For example, recently, Raven Protocol (RAVEN) conducted an IDO on Binance DEX.

If all this talk of ICOs, STOs, IEOs, and IDOs sounds like a confusing alphabet soup, I understand. They are just different tools to raise funds. The regulatory concerns for ICOs are lower than those for STOs and IEOs.

STOs, on the other hand, have created such a high barrier for entry that they have become unviable for most projects. In sum, we are in flux. And should you pay close enough attention, you can grab a front row seat and watch how new fundraising mechanisms evolve. Enjoy the view!

Governance

Remember school student council? Or think about how your office works. How are, or were, decisions made? There are probably some formal and informal rules. The latter is known as "politics." That is, governance, the way a group of people do things. In the context of blockchain, it refers to the set of decision processes or systems that allow a platform to make consistent decisions over time and as conditions change.

The governance must be flexible to allow for adaptation to changing circumstances. Yet it must be firm and predictable enough to reassure all participants that the platform is fair and stable—and can enjoy a long future.

As you may imagine, creating and agreeing on the rules of the platform is not easy, especially when many participants are involved. But such is politics.

This Book

In 2005, I had a good job at a well-known technology company. One day, while we were sitting around a table imagining the world in 10 or 20 years, we found ourselves thinking out loud about how smartphones and location-based technologies could transform our lives. The ideas we came up with felt crazy. At the time, they were.

The following day, a colleague asked me which of these ideas, if any, could come true. I shrugged my shoulders and sad, "It is hard to choose. They are all crazy enough that they each give me pause. And yet I feel that any and all of them could be part of our lives." Fast-forward 15 years, and now all those ideas we brainstormed in 2005 have come to fruition. What felt crazy then is the new normal in our society.

I decided to write this book because I am convinced that blockchain technology will transform our lives and usher in a new normal, especially in the next 5 to 10 years. In 15 years, I believe our lives will be unrecognizable to our current selves, largely because of the value and capabilities that blockchain offers.

For this reason, this book is not organized by industry. In fact, it makes no sense to organize a book about blockchain by industry any more than it would to organize a book about electricity by industry. Instead, this book is organized by added values that blockchain brings, values that we will eventually find ourselves unable to live without. Although those values and capabilities may be applied and monetized differently in different industries, they are ultimately constant.

Just like electricity can be combined with other technologies to light up, warm up, and energize objects across industries, this book focuses on the nonexclusive values that can be used across industries. To be clear, these are not exhaustive values but merely the ones that seem compelling enough to explore in great depth now. My expectation is that the values detailed in this book will further evolve and that other values not mentioned in this book will emerge or soon be explored further.

Chapter 1 explores how blockchain technology adds value to data management, security, and sharing. Chapter 2 focuses on Blockchain-as-a-Service (BaaS), a method for companies to take advantage of blockchain technology more easily and quickly. Chapter 3 discusses how blockchain technology may transform our understanding of digital goods or dGoods. Chapter 4 dives into ownership and property and how blockchain technology is changing both concepts. Chapter 5 zeroes in on how blockchain technology will change how we collaborate and how this, in turn, will radically change what is possible to accomplish together. Chapter 6 dives into trust and how blockchain technology redefines what it is and how to develop it. And, finally, Chapter 7 focuses on the transformative power of small acts and micropayments amplified by blockchain.

Let the blockchain technology journey begin!

CHAPTER 1

Stumbling upon Digital Gold: Tapping into Data's Potential for Management, Security, and Sharing

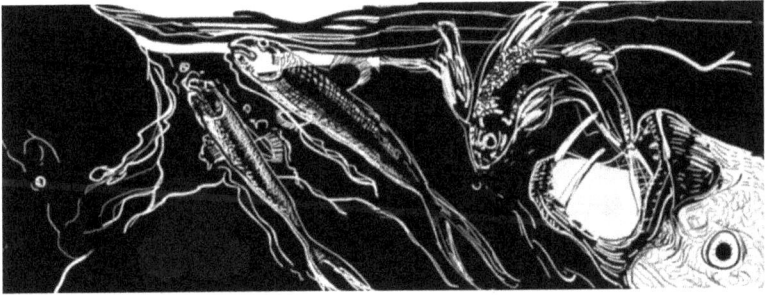

DADA Collective: Otro Captore, Chile / Massel Quispe, Peru.,
collaboratively created using blockchain technology, a visual conversation.

The Internet is currently a gold mine of data waiting to be discovered, and transformed into a usable form. The modern economy is data driven because data is valuable to employers and business leaders—it empowers them to make decisions based on facts, not guesses. Marketing departments use market segmentation data to identify new, eager customers. Human resources professionals gather data to recruit the best talent and verify their qualifications. Business executives examine macro trends to make sure that their products and services are relevant—and rely on aggregations to do so. The returns and savings on data usage are unprecedented and worth pursuing.

You've probably heard the term "big data" recently. It's mostly an imaginary category. There's no threshold that makes data "big." But the term is helpful because it represents the increasing volumes and the varied types of data that are gathered, as well as data's importance in our lives.

In the world of "big data," there are two basic types of data: Human-readable data (also known as unstructured data) is information that only humans can interpret, whereas machine-readable data (or structured data) is information that a computer can process. Because computer processing is cheaper and much more efficient than human processing, structured data is especially valuable to scaling modern businesses.

Both structured and unstructured data fall into at least one of the following four categories:

- **Personal data**—it is specific to you and includes information like your demographics, your location, your e-mail address, and other identifying factors.
- **Transactional data**—it is anything that is created when you undertake some action—and leave a footprint behind. For example, when you click on an ad, or make a purchase, or even just visit a web page, you are creating transactional data.
- **Web data**—it refers to data that you could pull from the Internet, such as data on what your competitors are selling, published government data, or even basketball scores.
- **Sensor data**—it is data produced by objects such as thermostats or cars in interaction with their environment. These objects are often referred to as composing the Internet of Things (IoT).

Sifting through the data noise and getting relevant, not to mention accurate, information is not a simple task.

As you can imagine, there is a huge quantity of potential data out there. Sifting through the noise and getting relevant, not to mention accurate, information is not a simple task. Numerous professions, books, and conferences are dedicated to collecting, organizing, and interpreting data. Moreover, data collection, especially of personal data, is highly regulated in most countries. For example, the complexities of European Union's General Data Protection Regulation (GDPR) and the California Consumer Privacy Act (CCPA) are legendary.

Blockchain and data is a marriage made in heaven! They really complete each other.

It turns out that blockchain and data are a marriage made in heaven! They really complete each other. Blockchain can help data develop integrity and quality, secure in a more systematic way, track more easily, streamline sharing, generate trust, and analyze in real time.[1] This chapter traces businesses on the intersection of blockchain and data, specifically, how they use blockchain technology to manage, secure, and share data.

---

[1] J. Collen. 2018 "5 Reasons Why Data Scientists Should Use Blockchain." https://bigdata-madesimple.com/5-reasons-why-data-scientists-should-use-blockchain-technology/; A. Sharma. 2019. "How Blockchain and Big Data Complement Each Other." https://hackernoon.com/how-blockchain-and-big-data-complement-each-other-92a1b9f8b38d.

Data Management: Good Data + Censors = Magic

Blockchain provides numerous advantages for data management. Blockchain's key characteristics, including decentralized control; a secure and tamperproof infrastructure built on cryptography, transparency, durability, and robustness; and confidentiality, make it an ideal supplement to the existing tools for data management. It has what everyone in data management wants: data with complete provenance. It shows who did what, when, and how, and is verified by all participants.[2] This is a timely trend, especially in the increasing reality and importance of artificial intelligence (AI) and IoT, both of which rely heavily on data.

Data to a More Sustainable Future

Meet Kat Leigh,[3] the founder of SmallScaleOceanAction (SmallScaleOA), a circular economy for coastal data. Kat aims to use distributed ledger technology to incentivize traceable, transparent seafood, as well as inclusive, low-cost coastal research on a hyperlocalized scale.

According to Leigh, roughly half of the world's seafood comes from the chronically overlooked small-scale sector, which employs around 90 percent of fishers worldwide. Roughly 85 percent of the world's fishers and aquaculturists live in Asia. Indonesia, with its many islands and long coastline, is an especially critical supplier of seafood to the rest of the world.

Leigh says, "The seafood industry needs cheap, yet reliable information to monitor their operations, inform zonal management, provide

---

[2] P. Frøystad. 2016. "Blockchains and Data Management." https://www.finyear.com/Blockchains-and-Data-Management_a36228.html. See also T.K. Sharma. 2019. "Importance of Blockchain in Healthcare Data Management." https://www.blockchain-council.org/blockchain/importance-of-blockchain-in-healthcare-data-management/; P. Bains. 2018. "Using the Blockchain to Transform Data Management." https://www.itproportal.com/features/using-the-blockchain-to-transform-data-management/; N. Kudikala. 2018. "4 Possible Ways a Blockchain Can Impact Data Management." https://www.talend.com/blog/2018/06/11/4-possible-ways-a-blockchain-can-impact-data-management/.

[3] K. Leigh. Discussions with the author. 2019.

A fine example of a small-scale fishing boat in the Philippines.

evidence of compliance, and identify risk factors and associated mitiga-tion/adaptation strategies." Yet data is sorely lacking.

SmallScaleOA hopes to completely transform coastal communities and the seafood industry. It can enhance fisheries and farm productivity and efficiency; zonal management and marine spatial planning; product transparency/traceability for government or business quality and safety programs, or certification schemes; and even provide access to insurance, capital, investment, and financial services.

Morning landing of tuna catches in the Philippines.

She noted,

The more I learned about the Southeast Asian seafood industry, the more I realized that it is really a global center of seafood production. Indonesia is the second-largest producer of wild-caught seafood and the third largest in aquaculture. The potential benefit that could be generated by doing work in that region is what attracted me in the first place and has kept me going since. If we want to make an impact, this is certainly where we need to take action.

Weighing and logging catch data.

Why is Leigh so persistent and eager? Why did she pursue blockchain learning despite the very high learning barriers? Simple—the problem is big, solving it will have a huge impact, and Leigh is passionate about the cause. She observes,

> It's also worth noting that 97 percent of our fishers are in developing countries. When you think about massive boats going out there and collecting huge tons of fish, that is not the lion's share of seafood that's being pulled out of the ocean. This has major socioeconomic implications. There are a lot of issues, too. One-third of the products are mislabeled. We have illegal unreported undocumented fishing (IUU) and human rights violations.

According to Leigh, most places don't have catch data. Plus, there's global warming's evil twin: ocean acidification, the decline in oceans' pH caused by carbon dioxide emissions. In the end, many of the ocean's issues are due to the connections between our food system and the natural infrastructure. Of course, the ocean isn't just getting more acidic; it's also getting warmer. Leigh explains,

> Even though the ocean has been absorbing some carbon dioxide, our planet is still warming up, and doing so at an alarming rate. It's causing a change in sea surface temperature. The oceans have been heating 40 percent faster on average than a United Nations panel estimated 5 years ago. The rate is unprecedented.

What if we could link data on these phenomena to the decisions that our businesses, governments, and communities make? Leigh explains,

> If we're going to try to monitor all these crazy, scary changes, we need to fix the gaps in collecting this information and being able to act on it. Especially in the most severely impacted regions of the world. What are the obstacles to this? If you're trying to measure ocean acidification, you don't just measure pH; you need to measure two out of the six carbonate parameters. There are lots of different ones.

According to Leigh, "It is hard to scale this type of measurement. If you want to do it all around the world all the time, you'd have to have tons of people constantly taking samples." Leigh jokes,

I don't even think if you deployed every single grad student, you'd be able to exploit their labor enough to get those parameters. Autonomous sensors for things like pH and dissolved oxygen are new; and all are really expensive. There are a lot of obstacles to collecting this information, which is unfortunate because it's so valuable.

Another problem is interoperability. The sensors that are used are often produced by private companies that custom develop products for specific research based on request. Leigh explains,

> If you're a PhD or a postdoc, you have your research question, you talk to a company, and they build a product for that one research study. Again, that doesn't scale well. It's extremely inefficient. These are also private companies that understandably seek to profit off their sensors. So they're not sharing information, and it prevents technology from moving forward.

Leigh's vision is simple, "What if we could break that silo down and actually allow these companies to share their information and move technology forward? What if we could combine different innovations together and allow them to be mass produced more cheaply?"

The goal of SmallScaleOA is to increase data-based decision making by incentivizing the sharing of the data used for making decisions. Leigh is convinced "DLTs can make this possible. SmallScaleOA can incentivize the collection and sharing of data. If we have data flow not just up the supply chain but across into other actors in coastal communities, that would be great."

What if data producers were rewarded for their contributions? What if each data consumer, in order to get access to that data, had to compensate the producer? That's the idea with smart contracts—you can specify the terms and conditions of the exchange so that the data consumer must satisfy the producer's terms. With this approach, you end up sending value back down to the aquaculturists and fishers producing the data.

Leigh continues,

> The whole root idea behind this is that data collection has value. You incorporate that value explicitly into a transaction. With this

data, you can start making decisions about the environment, about other businesses, about marine spatial planning and zonal management, and you start involving far more people in the process.

She asserts, "It's a specific change that you can make in this specific area in a specific community. And it is useful immediately."

You also need a team to process the data. That's where academics, research institutions, and other folks come in. Leigh explains,

> They meet the terms and conditions of producer smart contracts to get the raw data. Then they do the processing, and then they put their processed data back onto the blockchain so that other people can use that processed information. But every time somebody wants to use processed information, they must meet the terms of the processors' smart contracts. So, researchers, too, get rewarded for their work.

In other words, every time someone takes a piece of data and shifts or uses it, that change can be traced and rewarded. You start creating this ecosystem of interactions all built around things that are interrelated and connected. Leigh observes, "This can really start to shift things."

Leigh is optimistic.

> If we were to live in this world—in which data consumers always compensate data producers—we could have all kinds of new interconnections. We would get key fisheries and aquaculture data, chain of custody data, and traceability and transparency data. All useful for supply chain efficiency, for value-added marketing for certification schemes for health, safety, quality control and compliance measures, and more.

That is how SmallScaleOA is building a mechanism to incentivize coastal resiliency—through the value of data and the movement of that data.

According to Leigh, SmallScaleOA brings together the academic community, the seafood supply chain community, conservationists, governments, citizens, and more. You can have projects from different communities all feeding into a larger data economy. They will help translate data from one sector to entities in other sectors. The walls of the silo will collapse.

The big idea here is that data is valuable for these different players but needs to be converted between different entities for that value to be realized. Leigh illustrates,

> For example, you might care about the number of fish in this shipment, but I don't care about the number of fish in the shipment. You may care where the shipment came from or you may care how many people were involved in processing that fish. To have that data flow fluidly, it helps to have currency to encourage that movement.

Thus, it would make sense to have smart contracts written in terms of cryptocurrencies, although this is certainly not the only option.

In SmallScaleOA, using novel sensors and mobile phone applications, fishers and aquaculturists will autonomously and continuously send data to a decentralized ecosystem. To access data, consumers— such as other fishers and aquaculturists, businesses, local communities, governments, nongovernmental organizations, multilateral institutions, or academics—will need to satisfy the terms of the smart contracts dictating the data exchange. Data users can then make informed decisions at the level of the fishery or farm, community, country, or even world. Leigh is convinced that this will work. She explains, "Through the inclusive, low-cost, localized collection and sharing of data, SmallScaleOA will integrate data-based decision-making into our daily lives."

Data to a Healthier You

Data management using blockchain may also prove useful for for-profit ventures. For example, Ben Hwang,[4] chairman and CEO at Profusa,[5] a medical device and data company that is pioneering

---

[4]B. Hwang. Discussions with the author. 2019.

[5]More information about Profusa is available at https://profusa.com/. See also, "Profusa Closes $45 Million Series C Financing." https://www.prnewswire.com/news-releases/profusa-closes-45-million-series-c-financing-300696522.html; D. Muoio. 2018. "Profusa's Embeddable Continuous Biosensor Draws $45M from Investors." https://www

tissue-integrating biosensors for continuous monitoring of body chemistries, is actively exploring blockchain capabilities for data management. The company designs and develops tissue-integrated sensors and biosensors that help in the management of various health conditions by offering biofeedback for chronic disease management such as diabetes and healthy living and monitoring of real-time body chemistries.

Hwang is a self-proclaimed "blockchain novice" who realized that blockchain presents a huge opportunity to realize his vision. Hwang explains,

> Our health care monetizes an individual's health care information and health care data. We can change it and put people in charge of how their data may be shared with care providers and stakeholders. In other words, people can own their data. The individual can be in charge.

Hwang realizes that blockchain is a fundamental technology with broad application. It is transformative. Hwang says,

> We have developed a medical technology platform. We can sense in real time clinical-grade chemistry as one lives her life. We can do that accurately. We aim to measure what doctors care about to enable them to make an accurate diagnosis and, more importantly, create the real-time feedback to allow an individual to live their most healthy lives.

He continues, "Our device is not measuring steps. We measure things that doctors care about. We also measure in a way so that physicians know what to do with the value that our technology provides."

He explains,

> The challenge that we overcame is that the body understands what belongs in the body and what does not. As soon as you stick a little needle through the skin, the body mounts what's

---

.mobihealthnews.com/content/profusas-embeddable-continuous-biosensor-draws-45m-investors.

called the foreign body response against it. Even if a sensor still works from an electrical engineering point of view, the body protects itself from the sensor by depositing collagen and scar tissue around it. So, the sensor will report a value, but that value no longer is indicative of the physiological condition. You basically measure the condition of the scar tissue rather than what's happening in the rest of the body.

Hwang says,

Our technology has overcome the effects of this foreign body response. We inject the sensors in the skin via a typical hypodermic needle, not dissimilar to the experience of getting a vaccine. That placement is not that invasive. The body doesn't mind it being there. So, the sensors work for months and years.

Hwang continues, "An additional benefit of our technology platform is cost. The cost of our technology can be quite low. The data is acquired at a very high rate, but the need to replace components is not frequent."

Why blockchain? Hwang says,

If I have an ability to create a stream of information of our chemistry, the question of data arises right away. Currently I'm not in control of the acquisition of my data any more than I am of what the data does and where the data goes. I must rely on a health care professional somewhere. Today, I take a medical lab test and doctors give me an outcome. I have no control over that.

Hwang continues,

With the new paradigm shift ushered in by our sensor technology, the user is now the one that generates the data. That data is around the user as an individual, and she can choose to share that data with a care provider of her choice and if she wants to continue to share it with the doctor or not. When you change the paradigm to a patient-centered model, and the patient is the one who controls their data and how it is analyzed, as opposed to a hospital or system, the impact is profound.

According to Hwang,

One, the cost of care could be drastically lowered. Two, I'm able to get that information and create market efficiencies. You now have much more latitude to shop for services and to buy what you like or care about. You are no longer a prisoner of the bureaucratic system. Changing doctors can be much more painless.

Hwang says, "Blockchain will help with data security, data flow, and data control. In the health care arena, the benefits of blockchain technology are even more important, especially when we launch next-generation consumer health products."

Hwang explains,

We are still asking ourselves how to prove that in-home individualized deployment of our sensor data and integration of blockchain technology and data security can create data transactional value for the individual and the system. We are in exploratory phases. We are making pretty good traction.

The use of blockchain in health-related data companies is becoming more and more popular. For example, Gem[6] builds tools powered by blockchain to connect large and disconnected data sets on one platform. The company has developed an operating system GemOS to access, request, program, store, and authenticate data on blockchain. Other health-related data powered by blockchain companies are also active in the space. For example, Chronicled applies blockchain technology combined with IoT systems to supply chains to help improve traceability and accountability. Its solution is crucial in industries such as pharma.[7] Coral Health[8] leverages the power of blockchain to make personalized medicine possible. Blockpharma[9] uses blockchain-based technologies to fight drug counterfeiting by improving drug traceability.

---

[6]More information about Gem is available at https://gem.co/.

[7]More information about Chronicled is available at https://www.chronicled.com/.

[8]More information about Coral Health is available at https://coral.health/product/.

[9]More information about Blockpharma is available at https://www.blockpharma.com/.

Data Security

Blockchain technology may be used to store data of almost any kind in a secure and permanent way.

Although originally blockchain technology was designed for the purpose of creating a peer-to-peer currency (remember Bitcoin?!), the underlying blockchain technology has characteristics that are useful outside of just peer-to-peer currency. A permanent, secure, distributed database has numerous applications that have nothing to do with peer-to-peer currency.

Blockchain technology may be used to store data of almost any kind in a secure and permanent way.[10] This often makes data more valuable and commands premium prices. Thus, numerous companies are seeking to monetize the security aspects of blockchain technologies. After all, properly designed blockchains are cryptographically and mathematically secured. Brute force attacks are highly unlikely to compromise them.

[10]S. Palavesh. 2018. "Here's How You Can Secure Your Data with Blockchain." https://www.entrepreneur.com/article/318477; See also D. Gutteridge. 2018. "Top 6 Blockchain Companies For Keeping Your Data Safe." https://www.investinblockchain.com/top-blockchain-companies-keep-data-safe/; K. Sharpe. 2018. "Company to Store Healthcare Data on Blockchain Platform for Simple and Secure Data Sharing." https://cointelegraph.com/news/company-to-store-healthcare-data-on-blockchain-platform-for-simple-and-secure-data-sharing.

Could the shift from centralized cloud storage to distributed services occur in the near future? Would a shift from personal identity and data storage, by governments and private corporations, to blockchain identity and data storage be a logical next step? Let's explore some examples.

Using Incentives to Secure Data

Storj[11] is a marketplace for buying and selling storage space. It is an open-source project for storing and saving files that allow you to install and run your own node on the Storj blockchain. Storj calls these users "renters." For the less technically inclined, Storj offers ready-made file storage services. Storj calls these users "farmers."

This hybrid business model approach, of protocol-level offerings and more user-friendly proprietary monetized service or application offerings, is increasingly popular among blockchain start-ups and comes with some real advantages. By making the base software open source, they invite others to build on their foundation and expand their reach. This ultimately helps their service.

Blockchain can address the tragedy of the commons of data -- a situation in a shared-resource system where individual users, acting independently according to their own self-interest, behave contrary to the common good of all users, by depleting or spoiling that resource through their collective action.

---

[11] More information about Storj is available at https://storj.io/.

All participants also have incentives to maintain the integrity of the network by competing to offer you the best security at the most economical price. This is another popular feature among blockchain startups. The goal is to address the tragedy of the commons—a situation in a shared-resource system where individual users, acting independently according to their self-interest, behave contrary to the common good of all users by depleting or spoiling that resource through their collective action. Other data security solutions powered by blockchain proliferate. For example, Sia, or Siacoin,[12] creates a similar market of buyers and sellers of file storage using smart contracts.

Blockchain on Top of Cloud to Secure

Other companies are actively engaging with data security powered by blockchain space. For example, Cryptyk[13] recognizes that blockchain has some limitations. The data that can be stored is restricted by the number of computers that are participating. Cryptyk breaks up data into disparate parts and stores them on third-party services such as Amazon's AWS, Dropbox, or Google Drive. It then uses blockchain to track and reassemble those file components when requested. Their blockchain layer on top of cloud storage is spread across multiple services, making it highly unlikely that if the file storage service were compromised, a hacker could access anything more than meaningless fragments of data.

Sovereign Identity to Secure Data

Civic[14] protects personal identity by not storing it! It allows you to enter your identification documents into Civic's Secure Identity App and then verifies that information with a trusted third-party authority, such as the government. This trusted party merely verifies that you entered accurate information; it does not know your identity. The Civic blockchain stores only enough information to verify the validity of your identification,

---

[12]More information about Sia is available at https://sia.tech/.

[13]More information about Cryptyk is available at https://www.cryptyk.io/.

[14]More information about Civic is available at https://www.civic.com/.

health insurance, or other documents and nothing more. So when you need to prove your identity to an organization, you show your credentials on the Civic Secure Identity App, which verifies that you indeed have the valid documents. But, importantly, you don't actually give that information to the receiving organization.

Once verified, the data is hashed and turned into an encrypted code. This encrypted code, not the data itself, is stored on the blockchain. Thus, potential hackers get at most meaningless codes that cannot be traced back to your documents.

Finally, with blockchains, it might be possible to prove our individual identities by establishing trust among ourselves, without an authority such as the government. We would maintain control over our own identity and data. It may also be faster and more convenient as it would avoid having to deal with bureaucracies. Solutions like SelfKey,[15] TheKey,[16] Iryo,[17] Patientory,[18] and Guardtime[19] have been experimenting with giving you, the user and identity owner, control of your identity.

Global Transactional Model to Rethink Security

Then there are some very different approaches out there! Meet Steven Sprague,[20] CEO of Rivetz Corp. His company provides tools to increase the value of a subscription to any web service by leveraging the embedded trusted computing technologies to enhance identity, privacy, ease of use, and security.[21] Sprague says,

> One of the challenges with blockchain is that we cannot prove that the data stored on a chain is real. They're immutable. You know that this transaction was written on a certain day at a certain time with the blockchain alone. But you do not have any evidence of what the

---

[15]More information about SelfKey is available at https://selfkey.org/.

[16]More information about TheKey is available at https://www.thekey.vip/#/homePage.

[17]More information about Iryo is available at https://iryo.network/#network.

[18]More information about Patientory is available at https://patientory.com/.

[19]More information about Guardtime is available at https://guardtime.com/.

[20]S. Sprague. Discussions with the author. 2019.

[21]More information about Rivetz Corp is available at https://rivetz.com/.

data for the transaction was intended for. Moreover, while you know it was signed by a private key, you do not know that the person who signed was in control of that private key when it was signed.

He continues,

This is a foundation of my observation in blockchain. When you think of blockchain, it is really two systems. The first system is this immutable ledger, the distributed ledger technology (DLT). It is the ability to store information and know it hasn't been altered.

He also says,

The second piece is how to program a distributed ledger technology to send instructions to it. This relates to wallet and private key concepts. You, the owner of the private key, really are the central god of all blockchain. If an owner of a private key never sends a transaction, the blockchain does not do anything. You need the infrastructure to help owners of the private key control their private key, assurance that whatever compliance they were supposed to follow before the transaction was sent was completed.

Sprague explains,

You need proof that these pieces were in place. That's the core of what we do. How do you establish proof that when a transaction is constructed and when it's written or when it's signed by the private key, that that signature was only applied when the user intended? At the heart of our economic model is assuring those layers of compliance.

He continues,

There are a variety of different ways to do that on blockchain. For example, IBM enabled a permission chain. It applies traditional cybersecurity controls by controlling the server, which then owns the private keys. Then they just do normal old-fashioned enterprise cybersecurity to make sure that only authorized users have access to the server.

According to Sprague,

At Rivetz, we are applying that model on a decentralized basis. We wrapped the policy around the private key within the client device. By enabling protection of the private key within the device, it can be decentralized. We can apply policies to the key before the key is used, in your wallet.

He continues,

Think of it as a set of very simple rules. Right before you're allowed to go outside and play, you must put on your hat and your mittens, which is a rule set by mom. The question is, where can I enforce that? Typically, you enforce it at the door on your way out. In the case of crypto, 'at the door' means at the signing of the transaction. If you put a whole transaction together in Bitcoin and then you push sign, you send that instruction off whether you send it to a smart contract or to the script on a chain. Whatever is included in that sign data is what gets processed.

According to Sprague, what we need to do is to collect the information and the security prior to that signing. Sprague continues,

That is why we run the signing process inside a trusted execution environment. That trusted execution environment allows us to put a rule in place that says, before you use this private key, you must comply with certain rules. For example, you may need to type in your PIN, go outside to check with the active directory server in your enterprise, or follow some other rules established before the key is used.

He continues, "We record each one of those rules. This way every single rule has been verified before signing and getting validated on the hash. Then we take that resulting hash and we write it into the transaction." Why would we do it this way? Sprague explains,

Simple. Say we go to court to prove that I wrote something on a blockchain. The first time we go to court, all that happens is you take a standard off the shelf, a theory on chain. We stand up in front of the judge and we'd get out ether scan. The judge says: "Great. I see that as a transaction. I see a sign; I believe in all the math of Ethereum. Fantastic. Explain to me how you protect your key." "Oh, I have my private key," you say. Then the judge asks a very simple but stupid question. Prove it to me. And so how do you believe that this is the only copy of your private information. The data on the chain could have been written by anybody who had copied your private key. "Do you have a copy of your private key?" "Yes." "Where do you keep it?" "In a vault." "Is it possible someone else might have access to the vault?" "Yes." "How do you know if somebody does or doesn't?" "I have a surveillance camera at home." "Can we have a copy of the surveillance footage for the last 4 years?" "I don't have it for the last 4 years. Only for 30 days." "Oh, so you don't know if somebody has stolen your private key."

In sum, the data on blockchain is of very low quality. It's probably worse than most enterprise servers. Sprague continues,

> Now that we've done a series of policy controls around the key and written a half-second hash into the transaction, let's go back to court. I can prove the transaction was done on a certain day at a certain time. Again, the judge asks to prove the protection of your private key. You say: "The second hash is the result of these manifest of controls and here is a list of controls. These dozen controls were performed before the key was used for signing."

He continues,

> You checked to see the health and integrity of the hardware that protects the key. Have you checked to see that I was in control of that device? You checked to see that you were still an employee, that the device is up to the enterprise network. You checked to see that I was physically in a certain building. You checked to see whatever controls the owner of the private key wishes to have. So now, you can prove that this private key was under this collection of controls. You can find this transaction.

According to Sprague, you can prove, for example, that your private key is held in a hardware device, that it had proper protections, and that it was used by a designated person at a location that you are familiar with. Sprague explains,

> We think that evidence bound to the data will improve the quality of the transaction stored on chain and therefore the reliability that they are real transactions. It's kind of like having oracles as policies, but those oracles are applied at the client device, not in a smart contract.

He explains,

> A trusted execution environment is very much like a smart contract. Within the device, yes, but it's a measured environment. So, you know that that environment was running in the expected condition according to the quality of the measurements that were made. That's what trusted computing is, right? You would argue a smart contract is trust, protected by a different method.

> That evidence bound to data and increased to reliability would presumably increase its use. Take a smart contract as an example. If I have a result written on a chain by a smart contract, do you know for sure that the smart contract wrote the result? I can look at the contract and say, "Well, what logic was in this contract? What happened?" You can say, "Well, these ten things happened. They got added together to create a certain result." Now you can assert that the smart contract was processed. You have evidence. What we're doing is generating a second hash within the client device in order to prove that the controls that the consumer chose to add to the key were in place at the time of the key.

He suggests,

> This implementation will make blockchain real. All the data written by blockchain today is arguably "fake news." You have no evidence that the data is real unless you run up the permission chain. Our approach will increase the value of the data. If you cannot use the blockchain to provide a truth without also collecting a windows log file from the machine that writes the transactions, then that doesn't seem to offer any efficiency at all. The real value

exists when a transaction travels with its forensic proof of the quality of the key.

According to Sprague, this approach will change commerce. He says,

The beauty of applying policy-added devices is that it happens with incredible privacy. Think of it this way: if your child is going to have a medical procedure done and must miss a week of school, you can send a doctor's note to school specifying an excused absence. Then your child does not have to make up the days at the end of the year if she has got a passing grade. That's a model that we as parents all understand.

He continues,

The financial services area is approaching the world in a different way. They think the right answer would be to send the patient ID code of the child to the school so the school could log into the health care records, monitor the active care of the child, and make a real-time determination on an hour-by-hour basis as to whether the child should be in school. That is absurd. And, it is most definitely not secure.

Sprague urges,

We have an opportunity to move toward a global transactional model where depending on whether I'm sending value from Libya to Egypt or from Boston to Miami, the regulatory regimes will differ. We would be much better off with a permission slip-type model where we can say, "This is a transaction that was delivered to this financial service institution, and it had all of its necessary compliance completed before the transaction was sent, as opposed to afterwards."

Sprague argues that this fundamentally changes the way we bank. Instead of data passing through institutions and each institution applying its controls likely at the protocol layer, we should predetermine the controls and assure that we are compliant. Then the protocols just move the value around. That is the only way to move money in the current complex, global geopolitical regime that is unlikely to change.

Consequently, according to Sprague, the blockchain protocol makes almost no money. It makes a penny to move $1 million from point A to point B. But compliance, the proof of compliance, and the generation of the forensics—all the work that's done in smart contracts and within trust execution—is where the transactional revenue occurs. You don't pay for compliance. You'll pay for KYC. You'll pay for an Anti-Money Laundering (AML) check. You'll pay for a geolocation validation. The validation of controls prior to transaction sending is very important. Those are not part of the protocols. Those are part of the instructions, and that is where business opportunities to monetize are located.

He explains,

> Protocols should be relatively stupid. Protocols should be protocols. They perform specific functions. They can't do everything. They're programmed by instructions. The compliance is applied at the instruction level. They're compliance validators, both providers and validators. I think traveling with a transaction should be found in a brief report that states that all checks were performed based on a compliance list.

In Sprague's model, the payment doesn't have to be in cryptocurrency. Obviously, if you are paying in micropayments, cryptocurrency has an obvious advantage and enables additional functionalities. But the payments could be in anything.

Sprague suggests, "With this approach there's just more simplicity in all the things we do. With this sort of ownership and control over transactions, the big data for the user starts to be collected, but the user retains central control." He continues,

> Instead of passing our transactions through a central service, we instead can choose to add controls to a transaction from the central services. And so therefore we can switch services much more easily because the Internet of monies or protocol just moves the money.

Data Sharing

Blockchain can help facilitate valuable, secure data sharing.

Imagine if we had everyone's complete genomic information. We could find endless correlations and cures to many diseases that are currently deemed untreatable. So why are we not working on aggregating everyone's genomic information?

Well, besides various privacy-related and personal information regulations, many people are worried that this information will be misused. For example, they are worried that certain gene carriers may be penalized with higher insurance premiums. So, clearly, lack of information sharing can impede progress.

Secure Data Sharing Is Possible

Can blockchain help facilitate secure data sharing?

Meet Nebula Genomics, or Nebula,[22] an effort to address this very problem. It provides a private and secure way to learn what your genes say about your traits and ancestry by building customized reports on new variants, risk scores, and research. It also allows you to share your data on your terms and get rewarded for choosing to directly contribute to

---

[22]More information about Nebula is available at https://nebula.org/.

medical research and discoveries. Nebula promises that, "It's your choice if you want to contribute. And if you do, you will always remain anonymous. Enter the age of personal genomics without risking the privacy of your most personal information." The company is developing cryptographic techniques to secure your genomic data and enable transparency. It promises, "Whether it's law enforcement or researchers, no one will be able to access your data without your consent."

Understanding that the primary reason why people haven't had their DNA sequenced is related to concerns about privacy and control of their genetic data, Nebula believes the solution for private DNA testing lies in new technologies rather than new policies. Nebula is "developing technology to protect the privacy of your genetic data and enable you to share it controllably and securely." Here's how it works:

- Data Ownership: You are assigned irrevocable (permanent) ownership of your genomic data on a publicly readable ledger. This enables transparent record-keeping of all data access requests and permissions. The identities of researchers who access your data are immutably (unchangeable) recorded, which helps establish accountability.
- Access Control: Your genetic data will be protected against misuse, hacking, and unauthorized access through an encryption scheme that uses multiple keys between multiple, independent, nonprofit research organizations. This multiparty access control will ensure that no single organization, including Nebula Genomics, will have access to your genetic data.
- Secure Sharing: If you decide to share access to your genetic data, it will remain in a secure computing environment. Researchers will submit analysis pipelines that will be executed on your genetic data, and only the results will be returned to them. Furthermore, for some common computations, such as queries and genomewide association studies, we will deploy a homomorphic encryption scheme to enable computing on encrypted data.[23]

---

[23]Nebula Genomics. 2019. "DNA Privacy. A New Approach." https://blog.nebula.org/dna-privacy/. See also Nebula Genomics. 2018. "Re-encryption by Proxy and Homomorphic Encryption." http://blog.nebula.org/re-encryption-by-proxy-and-homomorphic-encryption/.

Similarly, Doc.AI uses natural language processing, computer vision, and securing data through blockchain technology to generate insights from medical data. You can launch a "data trial," a collection of health data on the platform, for a cause or for general purposes, and then data scientists build predictive models. In the end, you will get insight into your data, which you can share with your doctor.

In this future, in which control over biological data, including genomic or microbiome, is consumer-controlled, blockchain based, and AI powered, you are in charge and at the center of your data sharing. Driven by their personal experiences with the current medical system, Doc.AI is accelerating medical research and discovering personal health insights.

zk-SNARK, an acronym for "zero-knowledge succinct noninteractive arguments of knowledge," or zero-knowledge proof, is another way to address privacy and security concerns. zk-SNARK is a cryptographic proof system where a user can verify a transaction without revealing the actual data of the transaction. In other words, zk-SNARKs allow users to maintain private transactions while still validating the transactions according to the network's consensus algorithm.[24]

For example, using zk-SNARK when you buy a bottle of champagne next time to celebrate getting through this book, you don't need to show your driver's license, thus revealing your address, weight, and date of birth; the seller will know whether you are over 21, which is the only thing he needs to know.

Some companies experiment with zero-knowledge proof in the context of delivering advertisements online. For example, if ads can be delivered verifiably without identifying the viewer using zero-knowledge proof, we can measure the performance of ads more precisely. This way we can compensate publishers and other stakeholders on the basis of their accomplishments and actions much more precisely than we do today.

---

[24]C. Lundkvist. 2017. "Introduction to zk-SNARKs with Examples." https://media .consensys.net/introduction-to-zksnarks-with-examples-3283b554fc3b.

Innovation around Data Sharing Is in Progress

Meet Tatyana Kanzaveli,[25] CEO of Open Health Network,[26] a white-label solution using blockchain and smart contracts to enable consumers to control and monetize their health information, including lifestyle and socioeconomic information. Powered by AI and big data analytics, the platform enables rapid development of digital health offerings: mobile and voice apps and chatbots for patients, health care providers, payers, and medical researchers. Open Health Network uses blockchain to manage users' identities and consents.

Open Health Network relaunched in 2015 on the White House Demo Day.

> We have identified sample data sets that include disease, environmental, social, and economic data that is typically excluded. We have data from devices along with patient reported data and data from electronic health records (EHRs) and claims. This gives doctors a fuller view into what happens with the patient.

Kanzaveli explains,

> I started this company as a patient. I wanted to create a truly patient-centered solution. So I am building a patient experience management platform. It's like SAP: customizable, personalized, adaptive platform powered by AI, and is ultimately a patient-centric solution. It is a business-to-business-to-consumer (B2B2C) solution.

She says,

> Our goal is to enable you to capture and integrate lots of good data. A lot of your data has been imprisoned within the various apps and devices. I was looking at how the data is shared. You go to the physician with a bag of medications and numerous pieces of paper. If you go from one care provider, you add even more papers. Everything on the data-sharing side was very ineffective

---

[25]T. Kanzaveli. Discussions with the author. 2019.

[26]More information about Open Health Networks is available at openhealth.com.

and inefficient. The patients don't have any control. We asked ourselves, "How can we enable health interactions in a more meaningful way where you, the patient, are at the center and your doctors have more information about you?"

Kanzaveli observes,

We help health care organizations create white-labeled digital health offerings where patients can not only gather all health-related data in one place, share them, engage in clinical trials and research but also learn about their disease, manage medications, book appointments, etc. Everything is configurable, personalized, and adaptive: from the look and feel of the apps to content and features. We also create custom AI algorithms and integrate them within the framework. For example, American Heart Association (AHA) used our platform to create My Cardiac Coach app. It is used by over 6,000 people daily who had a heart attack. It is available in English and Spanish. AHA used a number of modules from our platform. You don't need to write the code to develop highly sophisticated apps, which means very rapid (days to weeks) app development timeline. We have personalization, gamification, and recommendation engines. Our core platform gives companies content management system as well.

She says,

This app has been expanded with the data sharing option, so now within the app patients can see the share option on the top right corner. Patients who have been using this app for years to manage their health after a heart attack now can share their data based on their own consent [revocable] on a field-by-field basis. That's the real use case of using blockchain for health data sharing.

Kanzaveli continues,

We are using blockchain for patients' identity and consent management. The blockchain portion of our solution is agnostic to a chain but currently resides on Ethereum. Our architecture can be moved to any type of blockchain. We made some architectural decisions to make it flexible and adaptable.

Other companies innovate around data sharing using blockchain technology in and outside of the medical data. For example, Medicalchain[27] offers a decentralized, blockchain-based platform to securely store your health records and share these digital records with doctors, hospitals, laboratories, and pharmacists, if you permit.

EncrypGen[28] is building a unique blockchain platform, or the "Amazon of genetic material," to enable people to share genomic data safely and securely on a new emerging market using cryptocurrency. Katherine Kuzmeskas, the founder and CEO of SimplyVital Health,[29] is seeking to tackle the inefficiencies around value-based care.

Conclusion

Data is a buzzword but is also the foundation of the 21st-century economy. Across sectors, enormous volumes of data are being uncovered and utilized to unlock possibilities nobody was even thinking about just a few years ago, from alleviating overfishing in Southeast Asia to mapping genetic illnesses. But, like any raw resource, data is only valuable when it is managed efficiently and shared widely. Unfortunately, however, the more valuable it is, the more susceptible it is to theft.

With blockchain, big data will be even bigger in some sense and smaller in another. On the one hand, as discussed in other chapters, blockchain technology allows for a more comprehensive, granular, better quality, deeper, verifiable, and broader data set that was not available before. In other words, we increasingly have better data.

On the other hand, security, privacy, and fairness concerns shift data ownership from organizations to "safety vaults" that belong to individuals. Using increasingly sophisticated tools, these individuals will be making decisions whether to sell or share their data sets in the marketplaces

---

[27]More information about Medicalchain is available at https://medicalchain.com/en/.

[28]More information about EncrypGen is available at https://encrypgen.com/.

[29]More information about SimplyVitalHealth is available at https://www.simplyvitalhealth .com/.

that will likely soon emerge. In other words, the ownership of the data is shifting from companies to individuals.

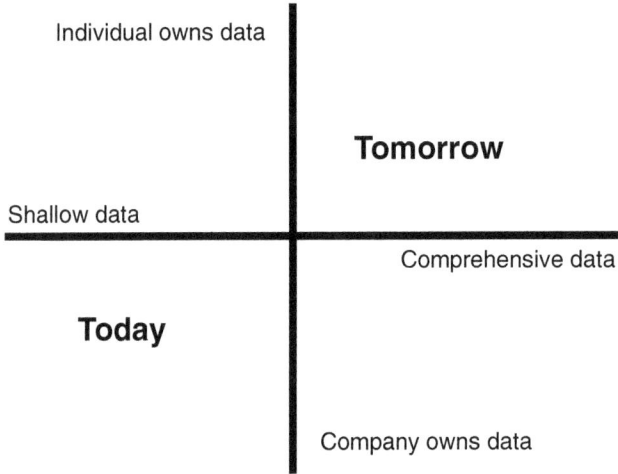

Individual owns data

Tomorrow

Shallow data

Comprehensive data

Today

Company owns data

The tradeoff between data ownership and data quality that is underlying the shifts in the Bug Data market.

This will fundamentally change the big data marketplace dynamics. The relationship between company and consumer will change because the underlying relationship and power dynamics will change. The companies will need to build even closer relationships with their customers and align their mission more intentionally to tap into the *power of the crowds*.

Simultaneously, we have been witnessing strong nudges toward sustainability, heightened corporate social responsibility (CSR), and increased value of privacy and security. The demand for *doing good at scale* is persistent and increasingly stronger. We have also been witnessing increased demand and expectation for transparency. None of these trends are particularly new, though they have been consistently gaining traction and strength in the last few decades.

Enter blockchain. Blockchain creates an infrastructure with complete provenance, recording a wide swath of information about each data to provide a holistic picture. As we can manage data more efficiently, there is no limit to the global puzzles that blockchain-based data solutions can address. At the same time, blockchain secures that data under lock and key. Thus, blockchain may be critical in building trust by design.

Yes, it's exciting to think of the medical advances that can be made if your entire genetic makeup is entered into a server, but it's less exciting when you think of possible outcomes when hackers get their hands on it. Blockchain will make that all but impossible. And, lastly, blockchain ensures that we can put all our data together to work toward technological advances together, rather than competing against each other in our own silos. When we can come together and share data, the results will be far greater than the sum of what we could each accomplish on our own.

DADA Collective: Boris Z. Simunich, Peru / Javier Errecarte, Spain, collaboratively created using blockchain technology, a visual conversation.

CHAPTER 2

Blockchain-as-a-Service: A Tale of Many Giants in a Crowded Room

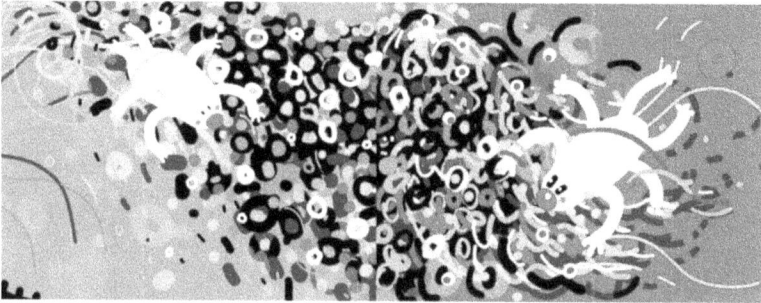

DADA Collective: Beatriz Ramos, USA / Otro Captore, Chile, collaboratively created using blockchain technology, a visual conversation.

Loosely speaking, Blockchain-as-a-Service (BaaS), sometimes also called Platform-as-a-Service (PaaS) or blockchain Platform-as-a-Service (bPaaS), involves the use of cloud tools and services to develop blockchain applications. Large companies like IBM and Oracle provide an ecosystem of tools for other companies to utilize blockchain technology. The final product often operates similar to more familiar platforms under those larger companies, such as Office 365, Salesforce.com, Google G Suite, Dropbox, or Slack.

BaaS often involves the use of cloud-based solutions to build, host, and use their own blockchain applications and software, smart contracts, or various other functions on the blockchain. The BaaS service operator often manages all the necessary features and activities to keep the system running and functional.

Typically, you, the end-user, subscribe to a specific package of an existing or new instance of software and pay a network fee or series of charges.

A cloud-based blockchain service often diminishes the complexities of implementation and allows you to master the blockchain technology quicker, on a more reasonable timeline, and with relative ease and greater guidance.

BaaS enables you to create and run blockchain applications with relative ease. Some question whether BaaS counts as blockchain as it lacks decentralization, often a critical element for blockchain services.[1] But regardless of whether it is considered blockchain technology, BaaS is critical for the widespread enterprise adoption of blockchain and may speed up the rate at which the technology is adopted and explored.

The Blockchain-as-a-Service (BaaS) space, right now, appears to be a small, crowded, and growing area in which well-known technology giants are positioning themselves to claim territory and acquire clients soon.

BaaS: The Breakdown

While you may be eager to implement blockchain innovations in your organization, there are several barriers to its widespread implementation. The technical issues and operational limitations are undoubtedly substantial.

---

[1] S. Radocchia. 2018. "Why Blockchain as A Service Solutions Aren't Blockchains." https://hackernoon.com/why-blockchain-as-a-service-solutions-arent-blockchains-8d588b1f35ce.

First, blockchain can be expensive. The cost and time commitment of setting up a full blockchain system is prohibitively high for many. As a small enterprise, you may not have the right personnel or enough resources to implement or maintain a blockchain solution from scratch. It is worth considering whether a blockchain solution is worth the investment.

Second, the use of blockchain technology requires expertise and a high tolerance for risk. A potential lack in either of these areas should be taken seriously when venturing into your first experience with blockchain technology through a BaaS provider.

BaaS promises enterprises a way to utilize the blockchain technology quickly and cost-effectively. More and more companies are taking advantage of these benefits by offering advanced products through BaaS because of its lower barriers to enter the field of innovation and as a way to facilitate the wider adoption of blockchain technologies.

Blockchain-as-a-Service (BaaS) mimics now common, standard, and accepted Software-as-a-Service (SaaS), Software-as-a-Infrastructure (IaaS), or Software-as-a-Platform (PaaS) models. These distribution models allow a third-party provider to host applications, infrastructure, or platform and make them available to the end-user over the Internet.

For BaaS companies, this provides an opportunity to identify or deepen relationships and partnerships with new clients, expand their product offerings, increase their revenue, and enter new markets. As a result, many well-known technology giants are reimagining SaaS to apply it as BaaS.

How Does BaaS Work?

Blockchain-as-a-Service adds an element of centralization to the blockchain. For this reason, blockchain purists argue that BaaS is not technically a blockchain at all but a more evolved distributed database. One commentator says, "It's a centralized product—buying it is just like buying a cloud service."

Because of this dimension of centralization, using a BaaS model enables you, an end-user, to focus your attention and resources on the actual functionality of the blockchain and the problem it is designed to solve, rather than the issues that inevitably arise when building a blockchain solution from scratch.[2] A BaaS provider often sets up, advises, maintains, and troubleshoots to make your blockchain adventures run as smoothly as possible.

The BaaS operator provides service support, algorithms, programming aspects, and numerous other services. It may also manage bandwidth, hosting, security, and many other features and functions. In sum, the BaaS provider handles the complex back end for you and your business. It is their responsibility to keep the platform and all the vital blockchain-related pieces running continuously and efficiently.

Many well-known companies and some start-ups are now providing BaaS services. From Ethereum-based platforms to Hyperledger-based, there are numerous BaaS offerings. In fact, the BaaS space, right now, appears to be a small, crowded, and growing area in which well-known technology giants are positioning themselves to claim territory and acquire clients soon. It is well-known that IBM has been heavily investing in blockchain generally and BaaS functionality specifically. Specifically, IBM is focusing its resources on private consortium blockchains. Likewise, Microsoft offers a BaaS module on its Azure platform. Amazon and Oracle have their own blockchain cloud BaaS hosting services.

The Linux Foundation, the Blockchain Switzerland

The Linux Foundation released the Hyperledger project, an umbrella project of open-source blockchains and tools that began in December 2015. IBM, Intel, SAP Ariba, and numerous other industry players support the collaborative development of blockchain-based distributed ledgers. Hyperledger integrates independent open protocols, frameworks, and standards for use-specific modules, such as smart contracts, consensus and storage routines, identity, access control, and others.[3]

In 2016, IBM and Digital Asset unleashed Fabric, probably the most popular blockchain framework, to Hyperledger. Fabric has a modular architecture that delineates roles between the nodes in the infrastructure, execution of smart contracts (called "chaincode"), and configurable consensus

---

[2]Ibid.

[3]More information about the Linux Foundation is available at https://www.hyperledger.org/.

and membership services.[4] A collaboration tool for building permissioned blockchain distributed ledgers, such as smart contracts, Hyperledger Fabric 1.0 became production-ready and has been gaining in popularity ever since. IBM, Oracle, and many other companies now offer services based on it.

Sawtooth, another well-known framework contributed by Intel, was also accepted to Hyperledger later in 2016. It contains a novel dynamic consensus protocol called "Proof of Elapsed Time." It also supports Ethereum smart contracts via "seth," a transaction processor. It includes Solidity support and Software Development Kit (SDK) for other programming languages.[5]

Generally, Hyperledger aims to advance cross-industry collaboration by developing blockchains and distributed ledgers that improve the performance and consistency to support major technological, financial, and supply chain global business transactions. It enables companies to create, manage, and operate a multi-institution blockchain network with ease. Notably, Hyperledger has not built its own cryptocurrency. To do so, Hyperledger has many other frameworks.[6]

IBM, the First Giant, Very Committed Mover

Early blockchain adopter, IBM Blockchain, offers a popular blockchain platform intended to quicken the advancement, oversight, and activity of a business blockchain network. It features access to the network's exchange administration, an authentication authority, and a network peer, running in an exceedingly secure condition and disengaged from other individuals' surroundings (extra friends can be bought for high accessibility) all to save your data. Its services are based on the open-source Hyperledger Fabric, version 1.0 from the Linux Foundation. It is a public cloud service that helps customers build blockchain networks.[7]

---

[4]More information about Hyperledger Fabric is available at https://www.hyperledger .org/projects/fabric.

[5]More information about Hyperledger Sawtooth is available at ttps://www.hyperledger .org/projects/sawtooth.

[6]More information about the Linux Foundation is available at https://www.hyperledger .org.

[7]More information about the IBM Blockchain is available at https://www.ibm.com/ blockchain. See also R. Miller. 2017. "IBM Unveils Blockchain as a Service Based on Open Source Hyperledger Fabric Technology." https://techcrunch.com/2017/03/19/

IBM Blockchain offers pluggable programming modules that can be written in mainstream programming languages, such as Java or Golang. It also contains security and secrecy controls to determine who can see them and who can execute them, a feature that scales and supports organizations of all sizes. Finally, IBM Blockchain shares blockchain use cases that help businesses identify possible opportunities where blockchain technology can be impactful.[8]

Reportedly, IBM Blockchain has over 1,600 employees working on more than 500 blockchain projects across industries. With so many developing partnerships, from universities to Fortune 500 companies, it is evident that IBM is betting big on blockchain. While IBM has projects in multiple verticals, it seems to be investing especially heavily in financial services, supply chain, and health care. It is also focusing on media, retail, and insurance. IBM is developing numerous tools from digital identity, food trust, payments, and many other areas.[9]

Microsoft Blockchain on Azure, a Close Contender

Microsoft Blockchain is another of the first and well-known BaaS platforms. Recently, Microsoft launched Azure Blockchain Service, a fully managed service designed to simplify creating and maintaining blockchain networks.[10] It is an enterprise service that helps businesses build applications on top of blockchain technology. Microsoft platform has no

ibm-unveils-blockchain-as-a-service-based-on-open-source-hyperledger-fabric-technology/.

[8]More information about the IBM Blockchain is available at https://www.ibm.com/blockchain.

[9]More information about the IBM Blockchain is available at https://www.ibm.com/blockchain. See also, Y. Khatri. 2019. "Volkswagen to Track Minerals Supply Chains Using IBM Blockchain." https://www.coindesk.com/volkswagen-to-track-minerals-supply-chains-using-ibm-blockchain; I. Allison 2019. "World's Second-Largest Grocer Joins IBM Food Trust Blockchain." https://www.coindesk.com/worlds-second-largest-grocer-joins-ibm-food-trust-blockchain.

[10]S. Colaner. 2019. "Microsoft Launches Fully Managed Azure Blockchain Service." https://venturebeat.com/2019/05/02/microsoft-launches-fully-managed-azure-blockchain-service.

cryptocurrencies. Reportedly, J.P. Morgan's Quorum, built on the Ethereum protocol, is the first to support it.[11]

The goal, according to Microsoft is,

> With a few simple clicks, users can create and deploy a permissioned blockchain network and manage consortium policies using an intuitive interface in the Azure portal. Built-in governance enables developers to add new members, set permissions, monitor network health and activity, and execute governed, private interactions through integrations with Azure Active Directory.

Microsoft is reportedly focusing on providing value to its existing partners and supply chain industry.[12]

At the same time, Microsoft has also launched an extension to its Visual Studio Code to help developers create and compile Ethereum smart contracts. The tool also allows developers to deploy smart contracts on the public chain or a consortium network in Azure Blockchain Service. Azure DevOps can then manage this code. Microsoft has two workflow integration services, Logic Apps and Flow, to help build applications for these smart contracts.[13]

Microsoft Blockchain Azure Service is a collection of Azure services and capabilities designed to help the end-user create and deploy blockchain applications to share business processes and data with other organizations. Microsoft Azure is a hyperscale global cloud platform that provides users with infrastructure services, such as virtual machines, storage, and networking. Its blockchain network is designed to be flexible, accessible, and user-friendly. Its goal is to make it easy for companies to deploy blockchain network topology in minutes with a single click.

---

[11]F. Lardinois. 2019. "Microsoft Launches a Fully Managed Blockchain Service." https://techcrunch.com/2019/05/02/microsoft-launches-a-fully-managed-blockchain-service/.

[12]M. Russinovich. "Digitizing Trust: Azure Blockchain Service Simplifies Blockchain Development."https://azure.microsoft.com/en-us/blog/digitizing-trust-azure-blockchain-service-simplifies-blockchain-development.

[13]Lardinois. "Microsoft Launches."

The Microsoft Azure platform is built around the Ethereum blockchain platform.[14]

Microsoft has been actively developing in the blockchain arena for some time now. In recent months, it rolled out Azure Blockchain Workbench, a set of blockchain applications on a preconfigured, Azure-supported network. Also, Azure Blockchain Developer Kit extended the capabilities of the Blockchain Workbench and focused on "connecting interfaces, integrating data and systems, and deploying smart contracts and blockchain networks." In the end, Microsoft is reportedly focusing on providing value to its existing partners and supply chain industry.[15]

Amazon, Another Contender That Has a Track Record

Recently, Amazon also released its own fully managed blockchain service: "Amazon Managed Blockchain is a fully managed service that makes it easy to create and manage scalable blockchain networks using the popular open-source frameworks Hyperledger Fabric and Ethereum." Unlike a Microsoft solution, it will support Ethereum in the future, for now, however, it is limited to Hyperledger Fabric.[16]

Amazon's evolution from a digital bookstore into a sizable online e-commerce store is one of the most notable commercial transformations of the 21st century. In the process, Amazon captured a good chunk of the cloud-based web services market with Amazon Web Services (AWS), providing cloud computing services for reliable, scalable, and inexpensive cloud computing services and along the way to becoming a real competitor to technology-centric data companies like Microsoft, Apple, and Google. It seems that Amazon Managed Blockchain is an increasingly

---

[14]More information about Azure Blockchain Service is available at https://azure .microsoft.com/en-us/services/blockchain-service/.

[15]More information about Azure Blockchain Workbench is available at https://azure .microsoft.com/en-us/features/blockchain-workbench/.

[16]More information about the Amazon Managed Blockchain is available at https:// aws.amazon.com/managed-blockchain/. See also, S. Colaner. 2019. "Amazon Managed Blockchain Hits General Availability." https://venturebeat.com/2019/04/30/ amazon-managed-blockchain-hits-general-availability/.

relevant BaaS provider. Currently, using APN Technology and Consulting as the primary pillars of its blockchain initiatives, Amazon allows companies to integrate their BaaS solutions.

Amazon BaaS integrates blockchain-based systems and commercial processes for some of the major companies in the world, including T-Mobile and PwC, to improve their IT infrastructure, business processes, human resources, financial transactions, and supply chains. Though it is still a work in progress, Amazon hopes that once your network is established on Amazon Managed Blockchain, it will be easier to manage and maintain your blockchain network.

Oracle, Yet Another Contender

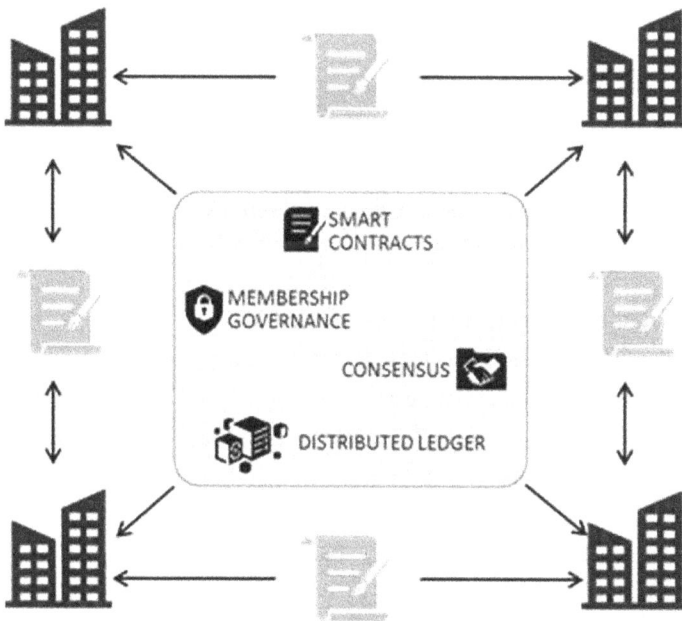

Oracle Blockchain Platform: hardened, pre-assembled, enterprise-grade cloud PaaS and on-premises offering.

Oracle is also considered a leader in the BaaS arena. It launched its enterprise-grade Oracle Blockchain Platform cloud service in 2018 after joining the Linux Foundation Hyperledger project in 2017 as part of its PaaS portfolio. Oracle also provides on-premises blockchain platform for customers who cannot deploy in Oracle Cloud due to data sovereignty, data residency, or other reasons.[17] Both the cloud and on-premises block-chain nodes can be used together in a hybrid network topology.

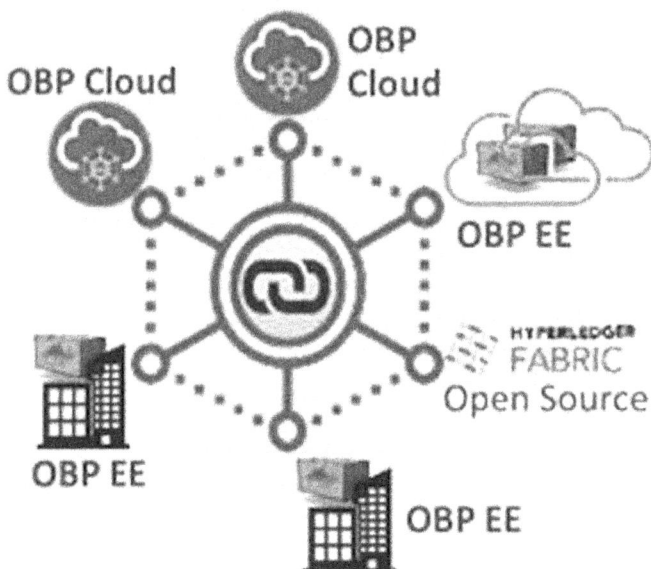

Flexible, hybrid, multi-cloud deployment options with Oracle Blockchain Platform in the cloud and on-premises.

Oracle Blockchain Applications Cloud is a set of SaaS applications built on the Oracle Blockchain Platform that provides business-ready applications that enable its customers to accelerate business growth by mitigating risks, creating new revenue streams, and reducing costs all at once. It was announced in 2018 to help organizations adopt blockchain technology and benefits in applications that range across industries and verticals. Its first solution released in June 2019 is Oracle Intelligent Track and Trace application, which includes an integrated supply chain track-ing application, smart contracts, design patterns, and templates to speed up blockchain integration across a trading ecosystem in supply chain networks. Additionally, it emphasizes both cutting-edge security and flexibility.

---

[17]More information about the Oracle Blockchain is available at https://oracle.com/blockchain. See more information about the Oracle Blockchain Platform at https://cloud.oracle.com/blockchain.

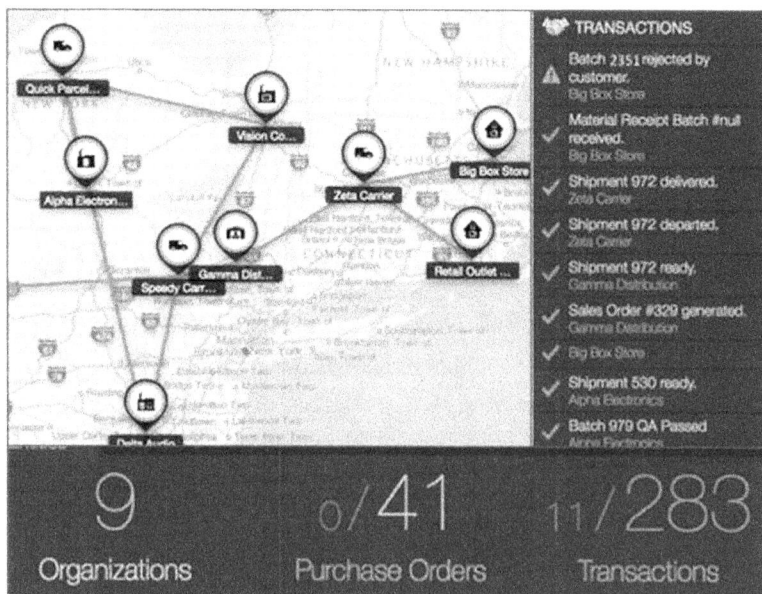

Oracle Intelligent Track & Trace: business-ready SaaS application for supply chain users built on Oracle Blockchain Platform.

Oracle Intelligent Track and Trace will extend beyond basic traceability with various features, such as lineage and provenance,[18] intelligent cold chain,[19] and warranty and usage tracking.[20] Oracle Blockchain Cloud Applications also leverage the Internet of Things (IoT) connectivity and use embedded artificial intelligence features to leverage real-time data to improve the accuracy of data.[21]

Oracle and Hyperledger Fabric Marriage

In writing this book, I interviewed Todd Little, Blockchain Platform Architect at Oracle Interview.[22] Oracle's goal is to encourage mass enterprise adoption of blockchain technology. Little explained, "Our goal is ultimately to make blockchain an enticing option for users. We believe in blockchain, and we're doing everything we can to spread the word." He

---

[18]Oracle Unveils Business-Ready Blockchain Applications. https://www.oracle.com/corporate/pressrelease/oow18-oracle-blockchain-apps-cloud-102318.html.

[19]Ibid.

[20]Ibid.

[21]Ibid.

[22]T. Little. Discussions with the author. 2019.

explained that Oracle Blockchain is based on Hyperledger Fabric and has improved functionality.

According to Little, "Everything we do is made possible by Hyperledger Fabric. It's a permissioned blockchain platform, and one that's highly modular where almost everything can be replaced." Oracle doesn't just utilize Fabric; it extends it in several ways. According to Little, Oracle's modifications will make it much easier to integrate blockchain technology. Little continues,

> We've made a bunch of enhancements to make it much easier to manage and monitor your blockchain platform. We've got a powerful console and DevOps APIs that take care of the administration. You can add new organizations, create channels, define policies, deploy smart contracts, examine the ledger blocks, and more through our console. We also provide monitoring dashboards for blockchain nodes and the underlying management of computer resources, statistics reporting, and topology visualizations.

Oracle Blockchain Platform: intuitive operations console with powerful administration, configuration, and monitoring tools.

Little explained,

> You can replace the consensus mechanism, you can replace the underlying database technology that's used, how membership is handled, and how identities are managed. You can replace pretty much everything within Hyperledger Fabric. All of the components are pluggable because of the modularity of Hyperledger Fabric. According to Little, smart contracts' functionality and

embedded certificate authority, which handles the issuance and revoking of certificates, are both critical.

We've integrated our platform with Oracle Identity Cloud Service so you can register and grant permission for people to participate. Also, there is what's called an ordering service, which is responsible for taking transactions and putting them in a specific order and then placing those transactions in a block and disseminating that block out to the other peers, Little added.

Oracle BaaS is provided as an Oracle-managed service. According to Little, "An Oracle-managed service means that Oracle takes care of providing the infrastructure in addition to monitoring and taking care of patching, upgrading, and backups. All of those operations Oracle handles for our customers."

A Heavy Bet on Permissioned Blockchain

Oracle focuses on permissioned blockchains:

At Oracle, we only focus on permissioned blockchains. Enterprise customers are dealing with their customers or their suppliers, and they need to know who those people are. The anonymity that public blockchain provides you with doesn't offer any value to a business.

He continues,

Our customers have to adhere to laws. And those are very difficult to do in a permissionless blockchain because you know nothing about who you're working with. Right now, there's only one suitable consensus protocol for permissionless blockchains, and that's proof of work. That is consuming an enormous amount of energy.

Finally, Little explained,

As Bitcoin continues to grow, the amount of energy being wasted even with simple commands is staggering. With permissioned blockchains, it is not an issue because you know who the parties are, and you can use other consensus algorithms that are much, much more efficient.

Consortium Appeal: The Value of Blockchain for Enterprises across Industries

According to Little,

> Blockchain is revolutionary because of what it allows companies to do. We're seeing the most significant interest in things like supply chains, tracking and trace, the provenance of information, and financial services. Making cross-border payments, invoice factoring, all those sorts of applications are going to move to a blockchain. And mainly because it helps increase the amount of trust between organizations and, in many cases, it's going to eliminate the intermediaries that just add cost and time delays to transactions.

Blockchain is adopted across many industries. Little says,

> We're seeing interest in everything from food and fashion provenance to health care to education to electric vehicles supply chains to loyalty systems. Our customers have an interest in this because of the increase in trust that is available through a blockchain.

Transparency is a vital blockchain feature. Little explains,

> For an enterprise client right now, so much is about transparency. With a traditional system, everybody's got their own silos of data. But with something like blockchain, we can come up with a single system of record that we use as the source of truth for anything that we're doing together between the two businesses. That's one of the significant areas—this transparency and trust that it facilitates.

Availability and security are other important factors. Little continues, "To hack a blockchain would require somebody to attack many nodes and basically subvert, you know, multiple nodes in a network. We're seeing that it also provides higher security for transactions between companies." Track and trace are also Oracle offerings. Little detailed, "Our customers use track and trace to make sense of information."

Consortium models are becoming popular among enterprises. To build a functioning consortium, legal and organizational requirements must be addressed. He explained, "These choices have nothing to do with the technology. You must show that there's independent value to doing this. And that's one of the more difficult parts."

You must figure out what the business value is. Little recommends looking for

> things like transparency, real-time reconciliation, being able to disintermediate your intermediaries so you can get rid of the banks—stuff like that is valuable. You must find those business values that are a key not just to that organization but also to the organizations that they do business with.

Look for the value blockchain can bring in a business-to-business transaction for everyone involved to find good uses of blockchain technology. Little explained, "We're focusing primarily on business-to-business transactions. If you are involved with blockchain, you must get some value out of it."

He explained further,

> You can't typically act like Walmart, who told their suppliers that they must put RFID chips on every package that comes in through their shipping warehouses, and now is telling their grocery suppliers that they must join its blockchain network. That's not going to work in a blockchain environment typically. Otherwise, you need a decentralized system because you need decentralized control in addition to decentralized technology.

According to Little, consortiums are generally challenging.

> The blockchain technology enables new business models. So, you must figure out how to apply those new business models and how to make them attractive financially. You need to have incentives for people to participate. If it just costs them and they don't gain anything, the project is going to be a failure. There must be motivation to be able to move to this technology.

Enterprises Tend to Start Small

Getting companies to start using blockchain technology may be a challenge. Little explained,

> We sometimes see customers have a hard time to start a pilot or proof of concept if they don't have a strong use case with business value because it could be difficult to get the C levels to fund it. It is still early, and we are still helping customers to develop spectacular use cases.

Little recommends asking a series of questions to make sure you use blockchain technology properly. For example,

> What are your possible friction points? What trust issues exist between you and your business partners? Where are you performing things like reconciliations are worth noting. That tells me right away that you've got two different systems and records that you're trying to keep in sync. Blockchain does that automatically and provides a good use case.

In the end, good use cases are obvious, not subtle. Little says, "Don't be frightened by blockchain technology. Also, test it. Finally, avoid the hype. When you find a good blockchain use case, it'll be clear to everyone involved that you found a good use case."

Abundance of Different Applications

Little shared many examples.

> One of our supply chain customers is Certified Origins. They're a producer of high-quality olive oil. They're an Italy-based firm, and they basically take care of working with the farmers to acquire olives, pressing them, and finally delivering them to stores. They're doing it using our blockchain service for their supply chain. From the time the olives are pressed into olive oil, they're tracking the lifecycle of the olive oil. You can scan the barcode on one of their bottles and get information about where the olives came from, like the name of the farm and processing plant. They now have this ability to give a lot more information to customers.

Certified Origins: tracking Bellucci Brand Italian extra version olive oil from pressing to consumer.

Another example:

CargoSmart, an information service provider and software developer for the maritime shipping industry, worked with a dozen global carrier companies and ports to announce and form the Global Shipping Business Network consortium. They've got some of the largest carriers and shippers and forwarders who are working together to put information on blockchain to create much more transparency and eliminate errors. For example, the carrier and the port terminal operators must know about the safety of the goods being shipped. Are the items dangerous (e.g., corrosive, radioactive, can catch on fire or explode)? Because if they are, they've got to be handled uniquely and placed in a certain part of the ship.

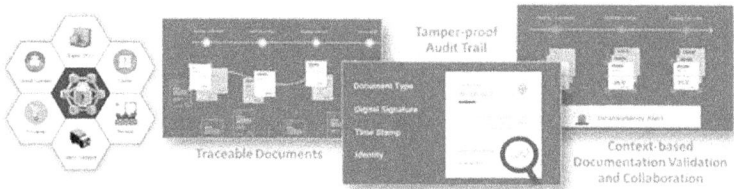

CargoSmart announced the execution of Global Shipping Business Network (GSBN) Services Agreements with maritime industry operators CMA CGM, COSCO SHIPPING LINES, COSCO SHIPPING Ports, Hapag-Lloyd, Hutchison Ports, OOCL, Port of Qingdao, PSA International and Shanghai International Port Group, with initial shipment tracking applications using a hybrid blockchain network spanning Oracle Blockchain Platform Cloud PaaS and on-premises instances of Oracle Blockchain Platform Enterprise Edition.

"There's a lot of back-and-forth between shippers, forwarders, and carriers, all of which must be tracked." He continues,

> They're moving to a decentralized document exchange that's blockchain-based, using blockchain technology to track all the information that's contained in these documents.[23] One of the reasons is that when there are errors or discrepancies in the documents, there are potential delays, extra fees, and fines. If the carrier or the shipper doesn't handle things properly it can delay the inspection and ship leaving the port, or container being cleared through customs. The customs or the port may impose extra fees or a fine on the carrier or the shipper. These blockchain records also help with a dispute resolution. So, it is advantageous for consortium members to have a single source of truth.

One of the reasons the supply chain is such a common use case for blockchain is that there are so many parties involved. According to Little,

> Multiple parties have a vested interest to make sure that things move smoothly, that the information is accurate, and that you can track and trace items. That's probably our most popular area. We're seeing interest across pretty much every one of our verticals. A single source of truth that all the parties can agree upon is generally valuable in the business world.

Another area is health care. Little says,

> One of our customers is using blockchain to track information about patients, especially around heart patients.[24] Relapses or complications occur within 1 to 2 weeks after surgery. Our client can collect vital readings on a frequent basis using at-home or wearable devices and share any abnormal readings on the blockchain monitored by the distributed care team so they can determine if an immediate response is required. Ability to provide and

---

[23]More information about this use case is available on Oracle blockchain blog. https://blogs.oracle.com/blockchain/oracle-and-cargosmart-teamwork-enables-broader-collaboration-across-nine-leading-ocean-carrier-and-terminal-operators-to-transform-global-shipping-industry; and in this case study: https://www.oracle.com/hk/customers/cargosmart-1-blockchain-cl.html.

[24]For more information see this case study: https://www.oracle.com/customers/healthsync-1-blockchain.html.

HEALTH⬢YNC + ORACLE'

*Healthsync deploys remote patient vitals monitoring and reporting
solution using Oracle IoT Cloud and Oracle Blockchain Platform BaaS.*

record an audit trail of near real-time notifications to all the doctors, nurses, and others participating in the patient's care is part of
the value of using blockchain.

He continues,

> Another area in healthcare that we're seeing its use is around access
> to confidential healthcare information. The idea is that you use
> the blockchain to mediate the access to information because our
> electronic healthcare records right now are somewhat scattered
> across multiple providers. Blockchain technology allows patients
> to control and authorize access to their records by various third
> parties such as medical professionals. We're also seeing similar
> trends in other industries.

Business process management software that integrates a company's fi-
nancials, supply chain, operations, reporting, manufacturing, and human
resource activities—software that are also known as enterprise resource
planning (ERP)—tend to be the place where a lot of reconciliations take
place, for example, between purchase orders and invoices. Streamlining
invoice reconciliation comes up often. Little explains,

> One of the big problems with invoices and purchase orders and
> the like is that each party has a different view of it. For example,
> if I order a bunch of goods, I may not get them all together, even
> though they were on one purchase order. Maybe it comes in mul-
> tiple sets of shipments. And if I have a separate system, I have to
> go through some sort of reconciliation.

> Blockchain technology can help keep track of it.

Neurosoft deploys invoice reconciliation solution on Oracle Blockchain Platform and integrates it with its invoice factoring solution Proxima.

According to Little,

> By using a blockchain, especially with permissioned blockchain, I can invite parties together, and we can then make sure, together, that we have a single source of truth. So that's going to be a benefit for any kind of business-to-business application because we no longer must have separate sources of truth. We can have one source of truth and eliminate the need for reconciliation.

College transcripts on a blockchain is another use, according to Little.

> With a blockchain, I might give somebody permission to be able to verify my degrees. And, they'd then be able to access that information confidentially. I can mediate that through a blockchain.[25]

Governments are also active in the blockchain technology. For example, he shared: Governments in multiple countries are planning to use blockchain to track permits and customs information for shipments arriving in and departing through customs agencies.

---

[25]See recent Oracle announcement of blockchain service for higher education community in partnership with N2N: https://www.cryptoninjas.net/2019/10/14/oracle-and-n2n-services-team-up-for-blockchain-based-student-verification/.

Specifically, it focuses on using blockchain to record and verify export/import permits, excise taxes, and tracking what kinds of goods and items are coming through customs to help streamline services and reduce fraud. [26]

Persevering through Numerous Challenges

There are of course challenges with blockchain technology. For example, interoperability within platforms and across platforms forms a significant and well-known challenge. According to Little,

> Interoperability is going to be a must. We may not have one dominant blockchain. If so, you're going to have to have inter-operation to make sure various blockchains talk. The problem right now is that we don't have suitable general-purpose proto-cols to do cross-ledger transfers. This is true within Hyperledger Fabric. It's also true between Hyperledger Fabric and Ethereum. We're going to have to solve this problem. But as an industry, we're still quite a way away from having the right solution to-ward interoperability.

Little also urged users to make sure that the problem you are solving does not have a simpler solution outside of blockchain technology.

> One of the first questions I ask customers is, what are the prob-lems you're trying to solve? What are the issues you're trying to deal with? Can they be solved with a centralized database? And if yes, we know how to build applications on those. We've been doing that for decades. Decentralized applications we've been doing only a few years. We don't have deep knowledge, we don't

---

[26] For more information see this conference presentation on Nigeria Customs https://static.rainfocus.com/oracle/oow18/sess/1525972961775001tGam/PF/Excise%20Trade%20on%20the%20Blockchain_1540245884923001J29M.pdf; and this article on government blockchain projects in Malaysia: https://www.asiablockchainreview.com/malaysias-mimos-partners-with-oracle-to-improve-transparency-via-blockchain/.

have the design patterns, at least not to the same extent as we have for centralized systems. That helps narrow down and eliminate wrong use cases.

Conclusion

Individuals and businesses are increasingly adapting blockchain technology for a variety of uses. However, the technical complexities still deter mass adoption, and the costly operational overhead in creating, configuring, and operating the blockchain and maintaining its infrastructure does not help. Along with well-known technology enterprises, many of whom offer favorable prices, many start-ups offer a viable solution to this problem through the BaaS model.

BaaS lowers the barrier to entry for the use of blockchain technology and may enable enterprises to experiment, evolve, and create better solutions. Soon, there may be rapid growth in adopting blockchain solutions for businesses. This will spurt an innovation drive that will influence possible use cases of blockchain for the benefit of industries as well as consumer ecosystems in the future.

BaaS seems to have numerous advantages. The predictable, low costs may give users an edge. For many BaaS providers, costs will generally be based on a monthly billing model, and they so far seem mostly affordable. Also, BaaS industry has the talent that can handle the underlying blockchain technology service. There are capable staff and developers ready to handle initial configuration and infrastructure maintenance.

In general, projects using BaaS can be rapidly scaled up or down with relatively low risk and at your own pace. Furthermore, there is a high level of data and information security. BaaS providers can pool resources to move and store data with far more protection than a company acting alone.

Yet, BaaS may have drawbacks. By hosting a blockchain on a single provider, you may wonder whether the benefits of centralization are worth the risks and whether you are truly taking advantage of blockchain capabilities. The data may be kept on the provider's property and governed by its policies. You may not own this network and may be required to simply trust those who do. You have limited control and, while dependent, pay more for these services. While upfront costs tend to be low, the long-term costs of using BaaS may be more expensive than self-hosting.

DADA Collective: Serste, Italy, collaboratively created using blockchain technology, a visual conversation.

CHAPTER 3

dGoods: Ownership and Assets Redefined

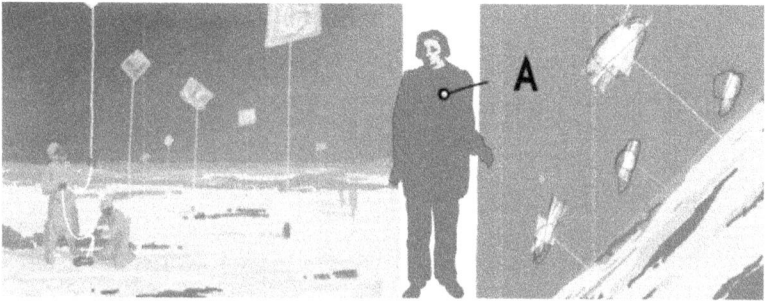

DADA Collective: Cromomaniaco, Chile / Otro Captore, Chile, collaboratively created using blockchain technology, a visual conversation.

Lost already? The bad news is, there are more unusual "cats" to come. The good news is, they will be fun, will challenge your imagination, and will extend your view of what is possible. And yes, you are in good hands to enjoy the process!

And don't worry if you partied a little too much in school and missed Economics 101. Together, we'll nail new up-to-date tech jargon and define money and explain why it's fungible.

Proverbially speaking, possession is 90 percent of the law. Though owning stuff has always been fun (just ask me how many shoes I own), with blockchain, ownership of assets can become even more exciting.

Cats throughout history.

New assets and new ways to own are now possible. This chapter focuses on digital goods or dGoods. Let's let the cat out of the bag!

Fungible versus Nonfungible: A Big Question

Fungible ERC-20 Tokens

To recap, a token represents a tradable asset or utility often found on a blockchain. Each token has specific properties that are defined to match its usage. They are both generic and fungible. In plain English, this means that a token can stand in for any form of value, and it is exchangeable between different specific types of value.

A token differs from our traditional monetary currency in that it is more generic. Whereas "money" represents specifically economic capital, tokens can define a broader set of values, including social capital, natural capital, or cultural capital. Simply put, "fungibility" is the essential feature of any currency, as a means of exchange, a unit of account, and a store of value. (And let's be honest, it's a great word no matter what it means).

A fungible good is defined by its type—by what it can be exchanged for. Each unit of fungible goods is not inherently unique, and as such is perfectly interchangeable. One $5 bill can be exchanged with another because they all hold the same value and are, for all intents and purposes, identical. A book that you pay $5 for cannot necessarily be exchanged for a shirt you pay $5 for; they are not fungible.

Brace yourselves—there's more tech jargon coming. Now that we know our fungibles, let's up the ante and bring in "fungible ERC-20" tokens. ERC-20 is a technical standard used for smart contracts on the Ethereum blockchain for implementing tokens. For our purposes, if you include certain functions in the token's smart contract, you are ERC-20 compliant.

Fungible ERC-20 tokens are interchangeable. A fungible token can be exchanged for any other token with the same value (like our $5 bill example). They are also uniform—each fungible token is identical to another token of the same kind. Like the dollar that can be divided into many cents, fungible tokens are divisible into smaller amounts, and you can send a friend a fraction of a token.

Other goods are nonfungibles. Whereas they may share common attributes, nonfungible products have unique traits and unique values assigned to those traits. Pokémon cards are a great example of nonfungible goods because whereas each one is unique, they all follow the same typology. Whereas one person may decide that one card is worth trading for another, that's *their* decision and *their* value judgment; the two cards are not inherently equal in value in the same way that two $5 bills are.

Because they are so flexible and interchangeable, fungible assets are commonly used by the crypto community and the fiat world today.

However, not all assets used are fungible. Nonfungible tokens (NFTs) are tokens that are uniquely identifiable and distinguishable during interaction and circulation.

Nonfungible ERC-721 Tokens

NFTs are rising in popularity, thanks to the emergence of the ERC-721 technical standard used for exchangeable, NFTs on the Ethereum blockchain. The ERC-721 standard is used to tie unique properties, and even real-world assets, to crypto assets. It sets forth a standard set of attributes and functions in the form of a smart contract that must be met to be managed, owned, and traded.

The classic technical standard ERC-20 is used for smart contracts on the Ethereum blockchain for implementing tokens. It covers only a few asset attributes, such as name, symbol, total supply, and balance. ERC-721, on the other hand, allows for more specific qualities. Applying this standard, you can now include rich metadata about an asset as well as information such as ownership. These additional details can ultimately add a lot of value.

Nonfungible ERC-720 tokens (NFTs) are noninterchangeable and cannot be replaced with other tokens of the same type. If you lend the token to someone, you expect them to return the same token. For instance, if a museum lends a Leonardo DaVinci painting to another museum for an exhibition, it wouldn't be too impressed if it received a Leonardo DiCaprio back. NFTs are unique, with individual attributes that make them irreplaceable or impossible to swap. Think of them as like concert tickets—while each ticket is to the same concert, each one has a different seat number. Furthermore, unlike our dollar, NFTs cannot be divided. In much the same way that your college degree cannot be shared or swapped with someone else's (which is a shame—how many of us really know what they want to do for the rest of our lives at that age ... or, in my case, at any age?).

The ERC-721 standards document an asset's ownership, approval, transfer, and other metadata. It enables you to record all your asset's valuable and conclusive information. For example, if you are a collector, you may value the ownership credentials of a collectible, provenance, and transaction history. Such additional information about your digital property may make it more valuable.

NFTs can carry unique types of information that make them rare and, sometimes, unlike any other token that's out there in circulation. If you have ever watched an 8-year-old play, fortunately, you will know just how much cache "RARE!" carries, and that's before we're even out of short trousers.

Fungible tokens may be limited in capturing and representing the value of goods that are indivisible and irreplaceable, such as a commodity, a contract, or a qualification. Conversely, NFTs can be used to represent unique goods such as a ticket, a bottle of wine, a piece of jewelry, and others. Tokenizing these unique objects of value allows you to trace the ownership, and in the process, you build a connection between information about the object and the value of the object. NFTs enable recording of the ownership of indivisible and unique assets, and an ownership record on blockchain makes the record transparent and tamper-resistant.

Applications of NFTs

CryptoKitties Fancies.

NFTs have interesting applications where unique digital items like collectibles need to be digitized. CryptoKitties, a popular Ethereum blockchain game, is a well-known application of nonfungible ETC-721 tokens (NFTs).

NFTs can be widely extended to collecting. For example, the information about an artwork, piece of jewelry, or any other collectible can be stored on the blockchain as an NFT. When you want to sell your van Gogh, you can list the NFT on an auction as proof that (a) your van Gogh is the real deal and (b) you are the valid owner. This traceable ownership prevents forgery and other compromises of the artwork.

Another highly practical use of NFTs is in authenticating the identity to obtain a full record of personal behavior. For example, you may own a token that represents your birth certificate, passport, or driver's license. Through access controls to these NFTs, the verification of your advancing years, your travels, and your traffic violations can be done securely and swiftly.

Another possible application is in ticketing. An NFT can represent a ticket to an opera or a soccer game to ensure that each ticket is valid and can be transferred.

As you are starting to see, NFTs have several applications, and we will look at some specific real-world examples.

CryptoKitties: Where It All Began

The first NFTs shot to prominence in late 2017 with the rise of Crypto-toKitties, an Ethereum-based game featuring thousands of—yes, you guessed it—digital kittens.

CryptoKitties Fancies.

When in Doubt Insert a Cute Kitten

CryptoKitties are collectible digital creatures on the Ethereum block-chain, and the only way to own them is to buy using ETH. It is the first consumer blockchain game, and each transaction in the game is logged and stored in the Ethereum blockchain.

CryptoKitties Fancies.

The rules of the game are simple: you buy a Kitty, breed to make more Kitties, discover new "cattributes" as you go, and build litters you love. The object of the game is to acquire cartoon digital kittens, each with their own specific attributes—sorry, cattributes. You can then try to generate kittens with rare characteristics by "breeding" them with other cats in their stable. When a new kitten is born, it inherits some of the cattributes of the parents, in addition to new, random ones. Each Kitty is unique.

You can acquire or sell cats in a marketplace supplied by the game. Today an eye-popping feline fortune of $25 million of Kitties has been bought and sold, mostly between players. Over 40 teams are creating more apps for the same Kitties, trying to grab some of that Kitty action. And there's plenty of action: at its peak, CryptoKitties was over 25 percent of the entire Ethereum blockchain's traffic, and the most expensive Kitty ever sold went for $140K to raise money for charity.

The scarcity of CryptoKitties is what makes it possible for them to be sold at such high prices. Ownership of these limited CryptoKitties is tracked via a smart contract running on the Ethereum blockchain. Each CryptoKitty's value can appreciate and depreciate based on the market, not unlike how the value of actual goods in actual markets works.[1]

By now you won't need us to tell you, but we'll say it anyway—the game is fun, and many got hooked. It's more than just cartoon cats built on blockchain technology, which would, of course, be revolutionary in itself. But trying to figure out the percentage chances of breeding a cat has spawned spreadsheets, apps, and communities. Chasing a specific breeding recipe to unlock a Fancy Cat is adrenaline-fueled entertainment. If you're a collector type, you'll want to complete sets of Fancy Cats, or perhaps create your collection of coveted Kitties.[2] (At this point, please

---

[1]E. Chen. 2018. "CryptoKitties and the Idea of Digital Scarcity." https://medium.com/dapp-pocket/cryptokitties-and-the-idea-of-digital-scarcity-4d2f83765463.

[2]CryptoKitties. 2019. "What the Heck Is a CryptoKitty?" https://medium.com/cryptokitties/what-the-heck-is-a-cryptokitty-4e14752e58c.

take note: we cannot take any responsibility for employee hours lost to CryptoKitties addiction.)

Interoperability Is a Secret Ingredient to Create New Attributes of Ownership, Scarcity, and Immortality

CryptoKitties Fancies.

An essential quality of CryptoKitties is that it is interoperable. Recall that CryptoKitty owners can "breed" two CryptoKitties to create offspring with new, distinguishing cattributes. And third-party services can be built on top of the CryptoKitties platform. For example, HyperDragons is a game where players can increase their dragon's strength by "eating" a kitten (ouch! sounds painful to watch). Even digi-nature can be cruel.

Dieter Shirley,[3] CTO at Dapper Labs which produced CryptoKitties, identified three critical NFT qualities that are prominent with CryptoKitties.

One, ownership. "You own your Kitty and can do whatever," Shirley says.

---

[3] D. Shirley. Discussions with the author. 2019.

This is very powerful—for people to own—because digital goods haven't been owned before. There are billions of possible Crypto-Kitty combinations. There's a perfect Kitty for everyone. Players can selectively breed to create their dream Kitty and can build collections of Kitties around any theme.

While it may look like a simple game with minimal functionality, "it demonstrates digital ownership of digital goods on the Internet in a way that is easy to understand for the less technically minded."[4]

Two, scarcity. Rules, transparency, and fairness are baked into the blockchain. NFTs can allow you to create real item scarcity. With CryptoKitties, each Kitty is unique, one of a kind, and with a distinct set of characteristics such as color, facial expressions, and fur. As we saw before, it's what allowed them to be sold for tens of thousands of dollars.

Three, immortality. Your CryptoKitty will likely outlive you. Shirley explained,

Kitties will live as long as the Ethereum platform is around. People love their cats. When you buy a CryptoKitty, no one can take it away from you or change it. Even if the CryptoKitties site shuts down, your cat will still exist as a hash code on the Ethereum network. A hundred years from now, you could gift your Kitty to your grandkids.[5]

dGoods with Humanity

CryptoKitties showcase the future potential of digital assets. As unlikely as it may sound on the face of it, if you own a CryptoKitty, you are a stakeholder helping to shape the future of digital assets, fostering camaraderie, and creating new experiences.

---

[4]T. Szikszai. 2017. "CryptoKitties Could Be the Single Most Important Application of Our Generation." https://medium.com/f0lio-cryptocurrency-portfolio/cryptokitties-could-be-the-single-most-important-application-of-our-generation-3f1a36212fbd.
[5]CryptoKitties. "What the Heck Is a CryptoKitty?"

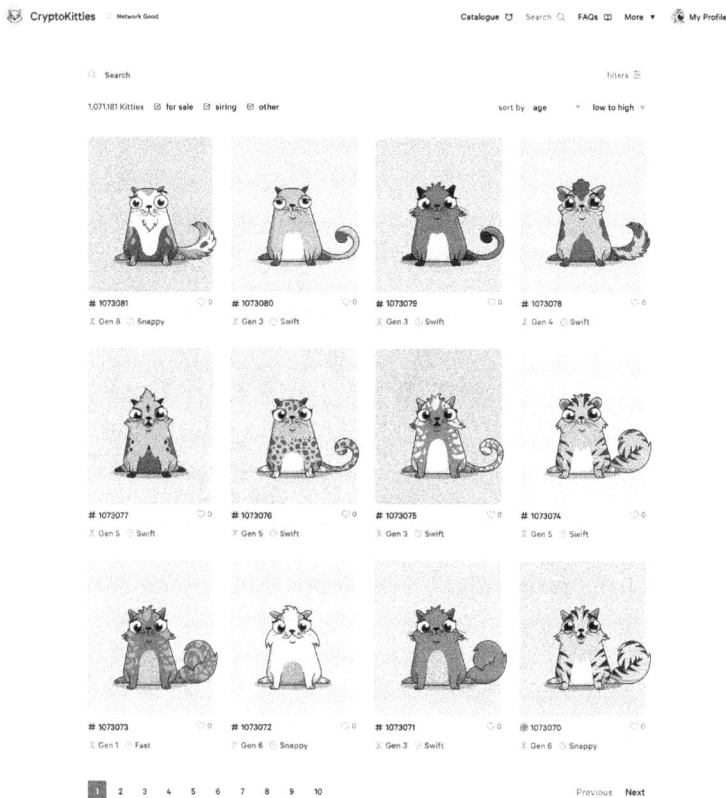

CryptoKitties screenshots.

Shirley explained, "CryptoKitties demonstrated that the NFT assets allow us to bring what we lost when we went from physical to digital. Now digital assets can signal scarcity, ownership, and status, and have the same properties as real-world assets do."

CryptoKitties also highlight that NFTs change how we transfer value. The Internet moves information quickly. According to Shirley,

> Just like e-mail is a base layer of the Internet, money and value transfer is native to the blockchain, and you can move money and value on blockchain quickly. People love that cats are meaningfully tradable assets, and this value transfer happens seamlessly.

Finally, CryptoKitties highlighted a new way for software to talk to other software. As third parties have been building on top of the CryptoKitties platform, it has become apparent that NFTs allow for software-to-software communication in unprecedented ways. For example, numerous third parties have developed accessories to add on to the CryptoKitties platform, such as hats for the Kitties (because every Kitty feels naked without one!).

Experiencing the Value

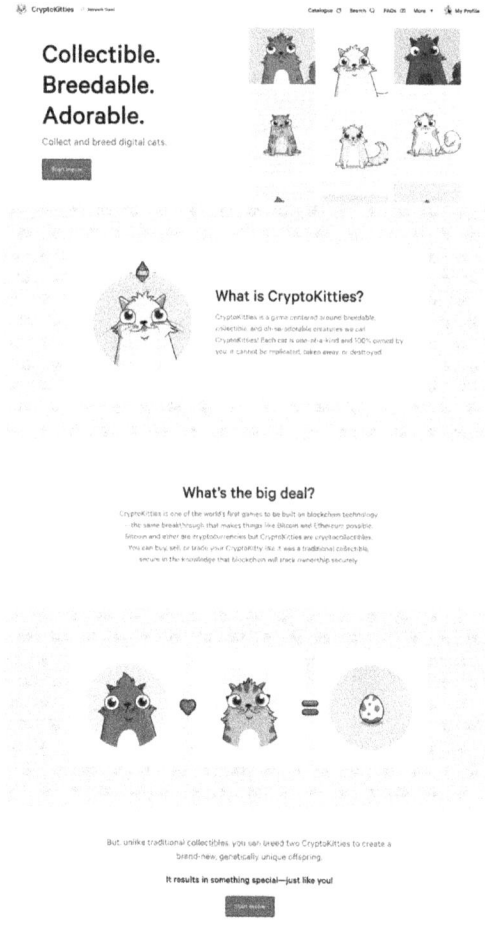

CryptoKitties screenshots.

According to Shirley,

> CryptoKitties is the first example of the value that people can experience. They were the first time that people could own something on the blockchain. Generally, when you play a game, you

only have the rights to use that character or that asset. You don't own those assets. With CryptoKitties, the rules are baking into the blockchain.

This notion of ownership is powerful on blockchain. Shirley explained,

Having these beautiful digital Kitties and knowing that they are yours is special. No one can take them away from you. As a result, CryptoKitties became the mascot for blockchain. It's something that people can experience. You can find cats as low as a dollar, and that's really what makes them accessible.
CryptoKitties has started democratized access to blockchain.

With CryptoKitties, 25 percent of our users were using blockchain for the first time. It wasn't just insiders; this wasn't just people in the industry who knew what they were doing. We made it more accessible and easier so that the average consumer could play this game and experience blockchain for the first time.

The CryptoKitties team was motivated to create something that people want. Shirley expands, Compared to other crypto experiences. We were not driven by ideology. We didn't want to try and make people understand what we're doing. We didn't write Medium posts, for example. We wanted people to come in and have it be obvious how to play the game. We were focused on a great experience for a user. We wanted a beautiful user experience, and we wanted to make sure that people want to own these assets. Shirley continued,

At that time there was so much jargon in this space and so many words that didn't make sense to the average person. And we took that out, and we replaced as much as we could with a "cat," something that everyone understood. That's what caught people's attention.

In the process, CryptoKitties also revealed a problem in the Ethereum platform. According to Shirley, Our funny little cat game overwhelmed the network. In December, a week after we launched, we represented more than a quarter of the transactions on the Ethereum network. We represented about half of the power of the theory network because our transactions are a little bit more complicated than just sending tokens around. And then, the price of gas—the price of the transaction costs of interacting with the network—went up by a factor of 100.

He continued, "

It was a terrible experience, and many people were angry. That was an eye-opening moment for us. It is not a coincidence that a month after CryptoKitties was released, the Ethereum Foundation announced that 2018 is going to be the year of scale.

Rethinking Our Business Models

CryptoKitties screenshots.

Shirley continued,

> A group of university students at a hackathon came up with Kitty
> Tinder. It's been incredible to see how that community is just con-
> tinuing to come together and layer even more functionality on top
> of our game. And because of the nature of a blockchain and smart
> contracts and the fact that the shared network enforces the rules,
> we can't stop them from building on top of our game.

Shirley observed, "Blockchain allows you to move services to an
open environment where no one can block it. The Internet had a rise
of open source and SaaS. You can create functionality like Facebook
using open-source software easily and quickly." He explained that NFTs
take this to the next level, "90 percent of the code that runs CryptoKitty
is open source. The value is in services. Closed services to open services
where people can combine. It would be transformational as SaaS was."

Shirley was surprised how much interest has been generated in building on top of the CryptoKitties. He observed,

> Before we launched, I don't think anyone on our team expected there
> would be this much enthusiasm to build on top of our platform.
> What surprised me was things like Kittyracing, which is a blockchain
> game where cats race around a little track, and someone wins the race.
> These people wanted to build a different kind of blockchain. They
> didn't care for CryptoKitties per se. And this was refreshing.

He explained,

> We didn't authorize Kittyracing. We didn't create the APIs for Kit-
> tyracing. We didn't even know Kittyracing was coming. We found
> out after it was already launched. We couldn't shut them down in
> any way, shape, or form. And that's amazing to me. This has the
> potential to change how software is written.

To increase adoption, Shirley believes that this technology will need
to evolve:

> For this technology to see mass adoption, it needs more interesting
> things to do. You shouldn't have to go through 25 different steps

to buy a hat for a game. We need to simplify the mechanics and make it easier and accessible for the average consumer because we don't see mainstream adoption until that's truly possible. And the last part is the capacity. There were numerous scaling issues with us. Scaling is the most important thing for us to see mainstream adoption. Our goal is to bring a billion people to the blockchain.

According to Shirley, NFTs bring specific physical world characteristics to digital assets.

Having a copy of a picture of an image, a jpeg of the Mona Lisa, for example, doesn't mean anything. Having a physical Da Vinci artifact means a lot. Blockchain lets us bring some of the things we lost in the move from the physical world to the digital world.

Shirley believes that, with CryptoKitties, we get to combine the best of the digital world with the best of the physical world. He says,

Baseball cards and CryptoKitties are easy analogies to make, but you can't breed two players together and get a third player that no one has ever seen before. And we can start to have things like scarcity, ownership, and signaling. The blockchain is like a crucial step in bringing back the best of the physical world and combining it with the digital.

Creating value in digital assets is critical, concludes Shirley.

A big part of what people love about their cats is that they are meaningfully tradable. They have value, and that value is what matters to people. Having the ability to transfer what matters to you over a digital network, I think, is a huge transformational effect.

Recently, Warner Music Group invested in Dapper Labs, creator of CryptoKitties, and a blockchain called "Flow." Expected to launch in 2020, Flow will permit users to buy and trade new digital merchandise, such as virtual posters and music, in real time across the globe. These and other projects demonstrate the exciting possibilities that technology and blockchain can offer the entertainment and sports industries.

From CryptoKitties to Video Gaming:
True Ownership of Digital Assets

Digital tokens can stand in for more than just currency. Game assets like game items and skins can be coded into tokens along with their unique appearance, characteristics, and histories. In this way, items can be unique, just like items in the real world, and the players can own their digital assets. If you have children, you will know that this is BIG. VERY BIG.[6]

CryptoKitties proved that people love "true ownership" of digital items, and it's easy to see how this idea can translate into the world of video games. If people enjoy collecting and breeding unique cats, imagine what will happen when unique characters and items with their histories and characteristics are available for use in popular video games (let me give you a clue—it involves money and lots of it).

Enjin Coin provides a platform for just this. You can use Enjin Coin to mint unique in-game items using Enjin Coins. Based on Ethereum, it is a collection of open-source smart contracts and software development kits that can be used to integrate blockchain into your games. Your players can even trade assets across other games that use Enjin Coin.[7]

We, humans, love collecting, whether it be stamps, pin badges, or baseball cards. In the physical world, such collectibles are the most common type of nonfungible assets. The issue with trying to transfer that to the digital realm is that collectibles can be copied and sent to someone else, diminishing their rarity and thus their value. By representing collectibles as tokens on blockchain, you eliminate the ability to double-spend and, in doing so, ensure security, ownership, and transparency around what collectibles you own. That is why many video game companies explore NFTs.

---

[6]K. Shilov. 2018. "3 Innovative Ways the Blockchain can Ramp up Your In-game Revenue." https://hackernoon.com/3-innovative-ways-the-blockchain-can-ramp-up-your-in-game-revenue-c00cc92c661e.

[7]More information about Enjin is available at https://enjincoin.io/.

The most basic kind of NFT-based game includes buying, selling, and trading unique tokens on Ethereum. For example, as we have seen, CryptoKitties allows you to buy, breed, and trade digital cats. It's no surprise that other animals have sought to get a piece of the NFT action. PlasmaBears[8] enables you to build, sell, and trade—wait for it—digital bears. You can send them on adventures to discover valuable, wearable, and tradable assets. Etheremon enables you to strike out and capture, train, sell, and trade unique digital creatures known as Mons.[9]

Other popular NFT-based games are battling games. Again, they are underpinned by the basic tenets of collecting and trading, but with the bonus of fighting. In Chibi Fighters, you can collect, trade, and digitally battle warriors on the battlefield, while weapons that kill and destroy in a multitude of deeply satisfying ways are some of the in-game assets that you can collect and trade. In HyperDragons, you can collect, breed, train, trade, and battle unique digital tortoises (ok, it's dragons) on the blockchain. Meanwhile, in Axie Infinity, you can collect, raise, and battle unique digital fantasy creatures.[10]

Another way that gaming has capitalized on NFTs is in strategy games. While still mostly collecting and trading games, they have included a little extra complexity for the more discerning gamer that seeks a more intellectual challenge. For example, in Decentraland, you can claim your NFT-based plot of land in this virtual reality world and prepare to build and trade assets. In CryptoBaseball, you can collect tokens that represent real baseball players, and develop your team to reflect real-world performance. Back to fighting in CryptoAssault, you can command armies in a 3D world, capture territory, mine resources, and battle opponents.[11]

---

[8]More information about PlasmaBears is available at https://plasmabears.com/.
[9]ConsenSys. 2019. "You Can Make Money Right Now Playing Games on the Blockchain." https://media.consensys.net/you-can-make-money-right-now-playing-games-on-the-blockchain-4fd151dd7360.
[10]Ibid.
[11]Ibid.

Cruising with Javier: A Story of Blockchain Racing

Battle Racers: Logo.

We will take a closer look at the benefits of blockchain gaming with someone who knows the industry inside and out. Luna Javier is creative director at Altitude Games,[12] a mobile and blockchain games studio in Southeast Asia. Altitude is developing Battle Racers, an arcade racing game on the blockchain. She breaks down the intimidation factor of using blockchain in gaming. "Blockchain is intimidating. There are all these buzzwords. It's easier if you think of the blockchain as a gaming platform, as just a new technology that you can use to build games on."

Battle Racers: racing.

---

[12]L. Javier. Discussions with the author. 2019. More information about Altitude is available at http://www.altitude-games.com/.

Javier explains that blockchain games are unique and have certain distinct characteristics. There are three that she identifies as especially critical.

1. Decentralization: "In traditional video games like World of Warcraft, you can play for a long time and have a super-maxed out character with all maxed out gear. You probably worked very hard and invested time and money into developing this character. But the data is all centralized; it's stored on their servers. If anything happens to those servers, whether accidental or the company decides to delete your account, then you lose a year of your hard work. That's just how it is. Now, imagine if you have a character where data doesn't live in one place. With blockchain game design, if you are building on Ethereum, you have decentralization. Some amazing functionalities and features also become possible."

2. True ownership: Javier goes on to explain that blockchain allows for very real ownership. "Still using the World of Warcraft example, you as a player don't own your character or gear. You are just borrowing them for some time. If the game company shuts down, your items are gone. If the item lives on the blockchain, then we have 'true item ownership.' I own this the same way I own a physical Magic: The Gathering card. If I bought a Magic deck of cards, even if Wizards of the Coast were to shut down, I still own the cards. I can do whatever I want with them because I bought them and I hold them. We have never been able to do that with digital assets before the blockchain."

She emphasizes that true ownership allows you to bring your characters and assets to another game: "Because you own this character, you can decide to play another game with it. So if I own my World of Warcraft character, I could bring it into another game."

"A blockchain item can be used across different properties, and we call that 'interoperability.' This is what the developers are excited about; we can collaborate and support one another. This was also not possible before. In the past, companies would never share items across games. They wouldn't even share items across their own games! Now, these blockchain items and characters are independent of the companies where they originated. And they have real-world value! I could sell my digital item to somebody else the same way I could sell a Magic card to somebody else. And Wizards of the Coast has no control over that."

3. Gamers as investors: "This brings us to another valuable characteristic. We are used to buying a console game and paying $60 upfront. Or in mobile games, you don't pay anything upfront, but you can keep paying for in-app purchases. On average, players pay about a $100 for a console game and about $90 for a mobile game. With blockchain users, based on a September 2018 report, it was about $200 per blockchain gaming user—approximately twice as much. People are spending a lot of money."

"Blockchain gamers are more like investors. They want to buy these items and make their money back. That's a different mindset to understand and cater for. A blockchain game developer has to design a game where your players earned their investment back. These three characteristics of blockchain we didn't have before on any other platform."

Battle Racers: fun with weapons.

Racing around the Blockchain

Battle Racers: race track.

Javier, the first female game developer in the Philippines, explains,

> We made Battle Racers like an old-school arcade racing game. You walk into the Battle Racers arena and see a racetrack. Just like real life, you bring the little car you built, put it on the track, and then race against other people. Like in an arcade, you're standing around with other players doing real-time racing. And we've added some extra ingredients, such as weapons. It's turning out to be more fun than we thought it would be!

Battle Racers: Hyperion parts.

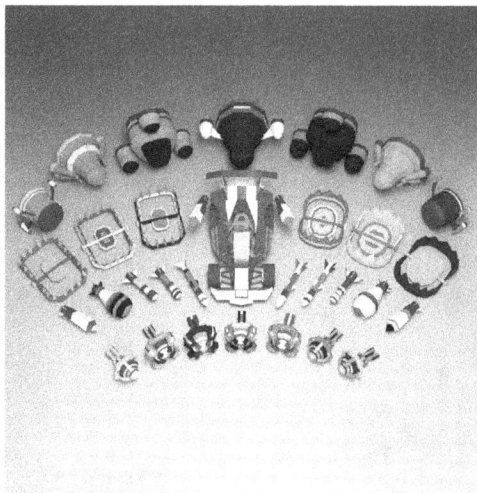

Battle Racers:collectable parts and weapons.

In general, a blockchain game must use blockchain technology in a meaningful way, and a really good game will use it to its advantage. In our case, the cars and car parts are ERC721 tokens. You can swap various parts around and mix and match to make a wacky car. And every part has different game stats—speed, etc. You can play in the arena for free without a car or play with a car you made but not tokenize it. Or you can tokenize them to become race cars.

Battle Racers: Vista.

Javier expands on the benefits that tokenization offers,

As soon as you tokenize a car, you can race on our competitive tracks and win real rewards. Your race car also starts to record history because it's a token. It is recording how many wins you have, who owns this car, and other information. You can imagine a car that's been around for 3 months and passed around from owner to owner. This car is getting older because you can't change the parts of the car and new parts are coming up all the time. It becomes vintage, famous, just like a car in the real world. And as you win with the car, you earn exclusive bonus stats that you can't get anywhere else. It becomes stronger, faster. The car becomes a legend and accumulates value.

Battle Racers: Hyperion.

According to Javier, tokenization is becoming the proverbial major leagues of gaming.

Blockchain keeps track of the increased value by etching history into the object. It becomes more than just a beautiful object—it now has another dimension of history, use, and users. It improves with age because it has experience. It becomes valuable because you can play the game on a different level and in a different way. If a tokenized car represents the major league, then a nontokenized car is kind of like a junior league.

Blockchain Tokens Enter the Sporting Arena

Let's turn our attention to the sporting arena, specifically to Michael Anderson who has entered the blockchain field of play with Hashletes. So what is Hashletes?

Hashletes formed a little over a year ago to solve the riddle of how to utilize a digital collectible in the sports world. Has it been successful? Well, it is now licensed by the NFL Players Association to build digital tokens for NFL athletes. So that would be a "yes."

Collecting Is Only Human

Real objects versus digital objects? That is the question!

Hashletes is a platform that creates digital collectibles (tokens) for athletes, ways to use them, such as games and content, and a place where users can trade Hashletes collectibles with each other. "This past NFL season, we launched the first digital collectible, a platform used in real money gaming," says Anderson.

What we do is we sell tokens related to athletes. These can be collected, they can be bought and sold on the marketplace, and then they can be used in real money gaming, somewhat akin to fantasy sports. We are working on new features and new capabilities for this upcoming season, and we're excited about NFTs and how they can be enabled in the sports world.[13]

According to Anderson,

Collecting scarce, physical assets—whether it be a hat, a jersey, a trading card—represent totems that relate to players and teams. They formed a meaningful bond between us and our favorite team or athlete. Unfortunately, digital fan experiences like fantasy sports have fallen short of replicating this meaningful bond.

As someone who loves her shoes (and no, I will never confess how many pairs I own), I can see how one of the biggest, most ingrained aspects of sports culture is the aspect of collectability. And I can certainly tell you all about the special bond my shoes and I share—especially when they speak to me as I walk into the store.

Owning Your Connections, Naturally

Nicolas Julia, co-founder and CEO of BlocSide Sports, the platform to collect and play with officially licensed football Crypto-goods, puts it into perspective:

When you think back to the Dotcom days, around 1998 to 2002, the companies that are still around today are platforms. It's the Yahoos, the Amazons, Googles, etc. We're going to see this kind of trend continues, but I also feel that the individual is going to become more empowered. One of the things I'm most excited about is sovereignty over our data. The blockchain enables new possibilities such as decentralized aspects and new data models. Sovereignty for data models is becoming important. And for it to

---

[13]NFT NYC. 2019. "Beyond the Bleachers—How NFTs Are Reshaping the Sports Fan Experience." https://www.youtube.com/watch?v=Db0ezRh3pYQ.

be sovereign, you have to be able to take your data away and take it where you want to take it.[14]

Julia explains,

One of the exciting steps that is going to happen is when you connect. Let's look at an athlete to a fan connection. Currently, you do that through a platform such as Instagram, Facebook, Twitter, etc., but the athlete doesn't own that connection. The ownership is with a third party or a platform. It is a little bit like the phone company owns your relationship with your neighbor. There are clear implications for this. If Instagram deletes your account, then those connections would be gone.

Social Spectrum: Not All Friends Are Created Equal

Julia continues,

The second phase is being able to start creating visibility around who's a more avid fan versus a general fan. When you think about an event at a stadium, how do you know who's in the crowd? How do you know if somebody is coming here because a friend invited them, or whether this is somebody who comes to at least three or four home games each season?

Let's look at another example, this time about a musical group. Julia says,

Consider a band playing their first concert, and each person that is at that first concert receives a badge. Now, let's say the band makes it big—imagine if they could identify the fans that have been following them from day one. We have new possibilities of creating something like that, allowing bands to determine who their avid fans are, who goes to their shows every time they're in town, who listens to their music and buys their albums and their merchandise and engages with the band on social media.

Julia observes,

---

[14]Ibid.

We see the first step in establishing these connections as enabling a band—or an athlete or a celebrity—to give some credentials for their social channels. That would start to identify who engages with their content the most, whether through liking, commenting, sharing things, reposting, etc. to create lists of what we could identify as "avid fans." Then there are some further clarifications where you want to identify not just obsessive fans, but ordinary fans who know and are into the band. If somebody leaves a comment on a thread on a social channel and other people like it, that's a signifier that it created or added some value to the conversation, as opposed to somebody just regularly posting stuff that doesn't matter. We are working through some of those things to bring that to the surface.

Just as we have different relationships with different people in the real world, close family, extended family, close friends, acquaintances, neighbors, celebrities can have different virtual relationships with different fans. Julia explains,

> That connection can be retargeted, communicated, and rewarded appropriately. So a band may want to do a free concert for all their avid fans because they're always buying their stuff and coming to the shows. It's tough to gain any visibility around that.

Rights Management, Amplified

Another area that is of huge importance to celebrities and athletes is rights management. Julia explains,

> NFTs have the rights management integrated within. If you tokenize yourself as a celebrity or an athlete you can create a parent and child relationship that allows you to do fun things like allow for somebody to play you in a game, as an avatar. Because you own that, now suddenly you can play that avatar inside of a game.

However, if that avatar is wearing a specific jersey, you're running into rights management issues with the team. Or, there could be other rights management concerns at a league level. Julia explains,

There is an opportunity to combine NFTs so you could have the player likeness or the person's likeness and the licensing of the team logos and league rights all combined and integrated to optimize the fan experience. If you could streamline these things, developers would be able to build on top of that without having to go through the process to acquire rights.

According to Julia, "there is a significant opportunity to streamline that process and foster innovation to build experiences utilizing blockchain." Julia explains,

I see blockchain removing the gatekeepers and intermediaries that typically create inefficiencies within that process. We are building a platform that allows for individuals, celebrities, and athletes to develop direct connections with their fan base. Then within those connections, celebrities and athletes can segment and identify on a spectrum of fandom.

Julia says,

We are working on solving that problem first. We're working on creating a platform for fan engagement where the athletes—or the brand, or celebrities, or the musicians—can create these connections with their fans that they own. In the first stage, we would start to aggregate through social channels to identify a category of fandom. We need to be creating these sovereign connections that don't have to be through the existing platforms, and then we can build on top of that.

Physical and Virtual Worlds Unite

Managing rights more efficiently, whether with fans or friends, can help the integration of physical and virtual worlds. According to Julia,

If you have a base avatar, that's a representation of the token, to develop this avatar further, you may have to go to a show or attend a game. Let's say you go to a game and you have a token of a player that beats a personal record or a league record, something like that. As those milestones are achieved, the avatar is changing. When the game is done maybe he has different shoes, jersey, skills, or scars. The avatar could have a new jersey, and you could take that and put it into a game environment and can play him. What if the gameplay is affected and it is different based on your activities? It creates a bridge between driving foot traffic and driving people to complete some kinds of tasks by having an impact on gameplay and creating a more virtual kind of environment.

In other words, it creates a seamless transition between the physical and digital worlds.

The integration of the physical and virtual worlds is, without a doubt, where we in the tech field are headed. For example, Amazon is now building or acquiring physical stores to help us integrate tangible, physical, and virtual realities, allowing the transition from one to another to be much more seamless. This increases stickiness and experience satisfaction. We see a bridge between the real and virtual worlds.

Conclusion

Some dGoods are also digital assets—they can themselves be assets or can reflect the ownership of an underlying asset. For example, electronic records that are the equivalents of negotiable instruments and electronic chattel paper would be digital assets, as would an electronic recording of a security interest in the underlying asset. It is similar to recording title to real or personal property and the use of tokens to represent revenue streams from otherwise illiquid assets such as patents and commercial real estate (sometimes referred to as a "tokenized" or digitized asset).

As we look ahead and try to anticipate the coming trends in technology, keep an eye on different types of digital possessions and how these assets are optimized, used, and monitored. Whether it's to ensure security against hacks or integrity to maintain value, all sorts of industries have a vested interest in improving the efficacy of how they own, store, and trade assets. As we have seen with the widespread adoption

and growth of NFTs, blockchain technology is being developed and utilized as solutions to problems that we didn't even realize we had. As our
digital assets continue to develop and become more complex, expect
nonfungible blockchain technology to follow closely behind, adapting
and constantly reproving its value as a source of innovation and creative
solutions.

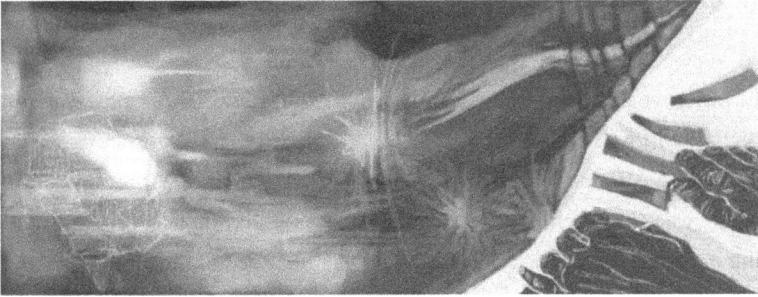

*DADA Collective: Lushan, China / Serste, Italy, collaboratively
created using blockchain technology, a visual conversation.*

CHAPTER 4

You, Yourself, and Your Stuff

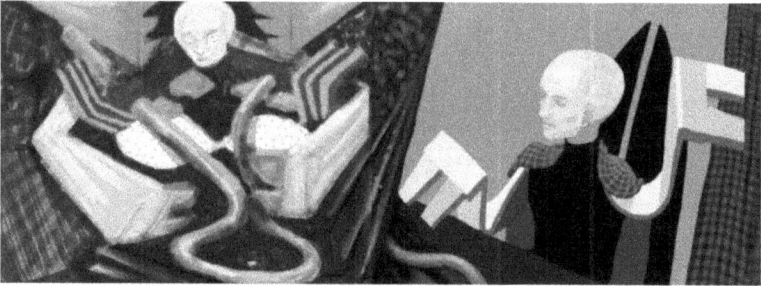

DADA Collective: Simon Wairiuko, Kenya / Boris Z. Simunich, Peru, collaboratively created using blockchain technology, a visual conversation.

"I should probably have told you sooner. I'm a twin. He lives in New York," my then-boyfriend of 1 month revealed to me as our airplane prepared to touch down at John F. Kennedy International Airport.

"I, too, have a New York twin. Give me a strong drink and a good New York party, and you'll meet a richer, carefree version of me," I teased.

"I have an identical twin brother here. He's fun. You'll like him," he replied casually.

We were only a month into our relationship, but I still wondered why he didn't tell me sooner. To every twin I had known previously, sharing a genetic make-up—and nearly every major life milestone—was a huge deal. It was central to their identity and typically a powerfully formative experience. Some felt a special, inarticulable bond; others were confused by the lack of connection they felt.

Digital Twins: Identity, Privacy, Reputation, and Social Network

Our digital twins to lead quiet, parallel lives in the shadow of our physical selves.

Fast-forward 15 years later, and it seems like we all have twins. Anyone who encounters the Internet has several digital versions of themselves—sometimes crafted, cultivated, and curated across various social and service platforms, but sometimes created accidentally in the footprint of our Internet usage. Data patterns—pictures, biographical facts, and online behavior—are transmitted increasingly seamlessly and efficiently between platforms, with or without our knowledge, and a cohesive narrative emerges.

These data patterns allow our digital twins to lead quiet, parallel lives in the shadow of our physical selves. Often, we are completely unaware for years and, in some cases, even decades. Your digital twins are complete profiles. They aren't merely a collection of a few random photos from your summer vacation or records from your latest online shopping spree, they are a comprehensive profile, including personal data that companies record outside of their own websites, in addition to data obtained from third parties.

Collectively, our digital twins have driven the growth of the Internet and the online platforms that provide services to us. These services—from Facebook and Instagram to LinkedIn and Amazon—are not actually free. By consenting to let the company own, use, and sell your personal information, you are selling them your digital twin. You trade them your most personal information for usage of their platform.

With ownership of your shadow self, companies then lend, sell, and otherwise monetize their version of you through advertising on a secondary market—all behind your back. And these companies know a lot about us. Facebook CEO Mark Zuckerberg confirmed many of our worst fears about Facebook's creepy and ethically shady practices in his 2018 testimony before the U.S. Congress.

If it sounds like George Orwell's Big Brother, it's because it is—but run by corporations, not the government. Thanks to an outdated and generally lax data protection regime, the ruling assumption is that companies own our digital twins. According to the laws, as they stand now, as soon as we click "I agree" after scrolling through the terms of service, our twins belong to corporations, with little legal obligations.

As consumers, we already have limited rights. But we need to become empowered and stop blindly accepting the terms of service and privacy policies that few read—and that companies write knowing few will read. We're all guilty of this. I'm a lawyer who used to write these policies, and even though I don't usually read them!

But our legislators have a responsibility as well. Right now, companies face almost no legal limits on what they can do with our personal data for their own profit. Our digital twins are theirs to do whatever they want with—to sell to a private corporation, a political campaign, even a foreign country. Lawmakers must return control of our digital selves to us, as well as broadly define our digital selves.

What if we could think of our digital twins as dGoods? Maybe, then, blockchain could enable us to own and organically track our digital selves? Maybe I could participate in digital commerce with more dignity and self-sovereignty—so that virtual transactions won't feel like a highway robbery?

Tokenizing Your Digital Twin to Improve Collaborations and Interactions

Is tokenizing ordinary people a future?

In Chapter 3, we discussed opportunities in blockchain for celebrities and athletes. This raises the question, why should athletes and celebrities have all the fun?!

Jodee Rich,[1] the founder and CEO of Kred and producer of NFT. NYC, is convinced that tokenizing ordinary people, and not just athletes

---

[1]V. Gupta. Discussions with the author. 2019.F. Arisandi. 2018. "Mattereum Is Unlike Any Blockchain Projects You've Ever Heard of." https://www.chepicap .com/en/news/5110/mattereum-is-not-the-like-any-of-blockchain-projects-you-ve-ever-heard-of.html. More information about Mattereum is available at https:// mattereum.com/. More information about JAAK is available at https://jaak.io/.K. Jackson. Discussions with the author. 2019.More information about Ujo Music is available at https://www.ujomusic.com. More information about Audius is available at https://audius.co/. More information about Open Music is available at http://open-music.org/. EY Global Leader. 2016. "Blockchain Reaction Tech Companies Plan for Critical Mass." https://www.ey.com/Publication/vwLUAssets/ ey-blockchain-reaction-tech-companies-plan-for-critical-mass/$FILE/ey-block-chain-reaction.pdf. S. Perez. 2017. "Spotify Acquires Blockchain Startup Media-chain to Solve Music's Attribution Problem." https://techcrunch.com/2017/04/26/

and celebrities, is the future. Admittedly, when he offered to tokenize me during our conversation, I felt a little objectified. *Thank you for offering to reduce me to a coin,* I thought. *That has been my lifelong dream!*

According to Rich,

> Blockchain is unique because it both exists everywhere and no-where. It lives on many, many servers across national boundaries all around the world, but is entirely decentralized. It makes it possible for applications like NFT.Kred to let people take control of their digital assets. For instance, an artist can send artwork to fans and followers for comment.

Rich highlights how little control we have over our "social currency"—"likes" on Facebook, for example—and how NFTs can address this. You have a profile on social media and create content, building a network through connections. And you have very little control over what people do with it—over your social currency.

Our identities sit in silos on Facebook, LinkedIn, Twitter. You don't have control. Over your newsfeed and over the format. You will also find it very difficult to download your social connections. According to Rich,

> NFTs are a scaffold that gives us control over our social currency. NFTs on the blockchain are immutable, so anything we put on it, no one else can change. It's decentralized, and it's stored, and we can control it with our keys.

Rich explains that in NFT.Kred, he has created a platform to put you in control of your social currency using NFTs. "NFTs tokenize social currency," says Rich.

> They carry identity, content, connections, and scarcity. NFT.Kred has created a platform that allows you, or any brand, to create your social currency. We can create your coin, card, badge, or any other token. We can take any digital asset, register it, and then trade it on the blockchain.

---

spotify-acquires-blockchain-startup-mediachain-to-solve-musics-attribution-prob-lem/.More information about Nuggets is available at https://nuggets.life.J. Roch. Discussions with the author. 2019.

Digital Scarcity in the Infinite Digital Universe

If you didn't feel objectified when Rich tokenized you with NFT.Kred, how you will feel when your social actions are tokenized?! First, let's look at what a social action is and why we would tokenize it.

Rich explains,

An example of a social action is a "like" on a social media post. "Likes" are ubiquitous. But if I give you a "like," you will still feel special. What I love about that is we all have this abundance of "likes," we have this abundance of content, but when we share it with the people we care about, they still feel special. And that's digital scarcity.

How did NFT.Kred solve the longstanding problem of how to let people control their network? Rich says, Brands and influencers allow their assets to be controlled by silos, big solid institutions like Facebook, LinkedIn, and Twitter. How do you give someone who is a big LinkedIn connector the ability to manage her profile? To have control over her contacts and then also to share her content across the network?

Rich explained,

Having worked with blockchain for years, a couple of years ago, we realized that we could take a coin that carries connections. If I give a coin to one of my connections and then he gave it to someone else, then the three of us would be connected. Now, if the coin had a topic associated with it, let's call it a review of your talk at a well-known conference, then it has some content, too. Everyone interested in this critical review would end up connected on that coin. We would immediately have a small network that would be topic-centric. As soon as you have a topic-centric baby network, you have an engagement. That is what we have done with NFT. Kred and NFT.Kred.

NFT.Kred uses this protocol to collect individuals' profiles, contacts, and content in one place. Not all of this data is put onto the blockchain, as Rich explains. "My vision is that someday, you will have most of your identities stored in the blockchain." In a world driven by competition, Rich concludes by highlighting the idea that ultimately drives NFT.Kred collaboration. "I think I can contribute and make money in the world by giving people a catalyst for collaboration. We build tools that allow people to work together."

Taking Back Control of Your Identity

Imagine not having to remember dozens of different username and password combinations for all the different sites you interact with each day. Imagine a world where you don't have to share the name of your favorite pet to pay your credit card bill. And for those of us who've never had a pet, I'm always tempted to use my husband's name because that's the closest I'd come to owning a pet before I had kids.

Forget all that and meet Nuggets, who will lead you to the promised land free of those silly dilemmas. Nuggets allows you to own all that information safely on blockchain and to protect it from security breaches or cyberattacks on those third-party companies. Soon, several large organizations in the United States, Europe, and China will be using Nuggets.

Enter Seema Johnson, co-founder and COO of Nuggets.[2] Johnson doesn't have a tech degree. Her entry into the world of tech was as a "project coordinator," where she learned the ropes and made the office coffee.

---

[2]V. Gupta. Discussions with the author. 2019.F. Arisandi. 2018. "Mattereum Is Unlike Any Blockchain Projects You've Ever Heard of." https://www.chepicap.com/en/news/5110/mattereum-is-not-the-like-any-of-blockchain-projects-you-ve-ever-heard-of.html. More information about Mattereum is available at https://mattereum.com/. More information about JAAK is available at https://jaak.io/.K. Jackson. Discussions with the author. 2019.More information about Ujo Music is available at https://www.ujomusic.com. More information about Audius is available at https://audius.co/. More information about Open Music is available at http://open-music.org/. EY Global Leader. 2016. "Blockchain Reaction Tech Companies Plan for Critical Mass." https://www.ey.com/Publication/vwLUAssets/ey-blockchain-reaction-tech-companies-plan-for-critical-mass/$FILE/ey-blockchain-*reaction.pdf*. S. Perez. 2017. "Spotify Acquires Blockchain Startup Mediachain to Solve Music's Attribution Problem." https://techcrunch.com/2017/04/26/spotify-acquires-blockchain-startup-mediachain-to-solve-musics-attribution-problem/.More information about Nuggets is available at https://nuggets.life.

It has been a steep climb for Johnson, and her hard work has paid off—she now finds herself as the co-founder of a leading blockchain company that has raised millions in an initial coin offering (ICO). Furthermore, she has achieved this as an Indian woman in the United Kingdom—and most impressively, while raising two young kids.

Nuggets has developed a blockchain platform that provides a single biometric tool for login, payment, and ID verification without sharing or storing your data. And the most remarkable is that not even Nuggets has any access to your data.

Say "No" to Honeypots of Data

Whenever we partake in online transactions, especially when we do our online shopping, we are giving out our information freely! We have usernames, passwords, and financial credentials saved across probably a hundred or more online locations. The problem with this is that all this information is being stored in these individual honeypots of data.

As honeypots attract bees, so does data attract criminals! Occasionally, data is compromised. You likely remember Equifax, Dropbox, Yahoo, and other major breaches from the headlines in recent years. And these are large organizations that spend billions of dollars on cybersecurity. *Great, even more people have my information*, is what I think every time I see a data theft headline. But I don't panic or lose sleep over it. Why? It happens all the time. The honeypot model is just totally broken.

We all love shopping online. We need to exist online, but how can we do so while ensuring that we retain our privacy and remain secure. If there is a data breach, we must change our details for every single location. That's the problem Nuggets solves.

The relevant term here is zero-knowledge. So what's zero-knowledge again?

It is one of my favorite terms in blockchain. It sounds like something straight from a Hollywood spy movie. In cryptography, this term is a bit more mundane. A zero-knowledge proof or zero-knowledge protocol is a method by which one party can prove to another party that they know a certain value without conveying any information other than the fact that they know the value. You don't need to reveal information to prove that it exists. A classic example is when you share your ID to verify that you are over 21. In the process, you reveal your exact date of birth and much, much more, whereas the bartender only needs to know whether you are over 21.

Johnson explains in numerous interviews,

We explored lots of other technologies before finding blockchain, but when we did, it was an epiphany moment. We realized that it not only gave us zero-knowledge storage it also ensured that there was no admin access or root-level access to the information. That's incredibly important for delivering a solution like Nuggets.

She continues,

It gave us the immutable ledger—simply a record that cannot be changed—ensuring that every time you carry out a transaction, whether it's a login or a payment, it happens successfully, and you have access to that information and no one else does. We needed the immutable ledger to be able to do that, and then we needed a high level of encryption that is inherent in the blockchain.

Another factor that Nuggets needed to consider is transaction speeds, an essential feature in delivering an e-commerce solution.

We are using a private blockchain. In a nutshell, when you download a product, you sign up is with your biometrics. It's whatever biometrics there are on a device, whether it's iOS or Android, and then it writes a private key that is the only private key. Then you take a still picture of yourself followed by a moving image to confirm your identity. It's like a moving selfie to make sure that the picture on the ID matches your face. Then you take a picture of a credit or debit card, and we check all that information. We do a forensic check on the card, and then all your data is encrypted on your mobile device.

She continues,

Once it goes to the blocks in the blockchain, then all of this is covered via another privacy framework that ensures that only you, and nobody else, can see any of the information that's in there. We

need to protect the user, and we don't have any back-door access to that then when we integrate with merchants. We've developed APIs that work with a lot of existing e-commerce platforms like Shopify, Magento, and others. Something crucial about Nuggets is that we're aiming at the mass market. Everyone shops online, and that means Nuggets can be valuable to a lot of people. A ton of those sites are built on Magento, Shopify, and their market-places. So we work with the merchants as well.
It is at this point that information is tokenized.

When you authorize, whether it is a login or a payment, that in-formation is tokenized, and only a minimal amount of data goes to the relevant organization. For example, if it's logistics, such as updatable information on your package delivery, then that goes directly to the logistics team rather than to everyone on the chain. I think that's important to remember about the Nugget solution.

Nuggets offers login, e-commerce payment, and ID verification, and when consumers use it, they are rewarded in "Nugs," a virtual currency that can be accrued. Johnson compares it to a loyalty scheme. On the merchant's side, integrating with Nuggets solves several critical issues. Johnson explains, "We all know data is critical. The ways we keep infor-mation are just not working."

So Why Own Your Digital Twin?

So why? Why own your digital twin? My hope is that you answer this question with a "duh, who *wouldn't* want to own extensions of their self?!" and an eye roll. There are at least five main reasons that we should have ownership over our digital selves.

First, our digital twins are an extension of ourselves. They reflect who we are as individuals, how we spend our time, who and what we like and dislike, our preferences and quirks. That's because we use the Internet for just about everything and our lives are increasingly digital and virtual. The idea that when we use the Internet, we consent to the use of the data we input is outdated. It made sense when we went online for just a few things: shopping, booking flights, even e-mailing. But today, we use the Internet for just about everything. It's an extension of our physical space, our physical reality, and it mediates much, if not most, of our very existence. In fact, in 2019, you can hardly function as an active member of our society without the Internet. Our digital twin, then, captures not just our marketing demographics or preferences but all of what makes us human.

It only makes sense that we have agency over our digital selves, just like we have agency over our physical selves or even our intellectual property. Why should a company's collection, aggregation, or manipulation of data about us change the ownership or create new rights? When you take a picture of Picasso's artwork, it's still his art. That you just snapped a quick picture doesn't mean you now own the image. Similarly, when you tell a friend a deeply personal secret, it's still your secret. You would never expect that they would spread it—sell it, even—and claim that it became their information to share when you divulged it. Why should the way we think about our digital information be any different?

Second, our control over our digital twin is an inalienable right, up there with "life, liberty, and the pursuit of happiness." We can work every day, albeit for very long hours, but we can never be expected to surrender our liberty. No matter what the employer asks, we have the right to walk away at any time, subject to the terms of contract, but never with the prospect of losing our liberty hanging over our heads. Most of us exchange our time for a paycheck, and in doing so, voluntarily give up certain luxuries—waking up at noon or taking a 2-hour mid-day nap. But we are not legally forced to surrender our very liberty or right to self-hood to our employers. Our employers can't jail us or enslave us. They can never own us.

Similarly, each of us should have control over our digital twins, even after we permit companies to use them in a defined way—just as we permit our employers to use our physical selves in a defined way. Selling our digital twins should be no more enforceable than selling our selves. It should be negotiated, equitable, and entered freely.

Third, clear, inalienable, individual ownership of our digital twins will encourage the development of more sophisticated technologies to keep track of and manage our digital twins. Companies will be forced to compete in the creation and use of these technologies, and consumers will enjoy more choices of social platforms with different technologies and policies, and ultimately better services and more options.

Today, there is essentially no competition or incentive for companies to innovate in social platforms. If you read a company's terms of service and privacy policy, disagree and refuse to consent, what are your alternatives? You will be left behind in the digital revolution. If you're a small company, and you don't want to hand over your digital self to Facebook, you technically have the right to refuse their terms and not use their service. But without access to the most widely used sales and advertising platform, your business will not be able to survive, much less compete. Have you noticed that a meaningful alternative to LinkedIn, Facebook, or Amazon does not exist? Where would you go if LinkedIn one day decided to cancel your profile in the middle of a grueling job search? Would it not be devastating? Where else would employers find you?

Fourth, if we do establish clear, inalienable, individual ownership of our digital twins, we will encourage the development of meaningful alternatives to existing services. The main reason for such high barriers to entry for possible alternatives to these social platforms and services is that each existing company already controls so much territory and information. Each company is a monopoly in its own area, owning every part of our digital twin.

Any person who wants to enter the market by creating an alternative will have to start from scratch—and immediately compete with an established giant. And our profiles are not portable. Users cannot move their connections, activities, or comments to a competition platform or service in any meaningful or efficient way, even if one existed.

And fifth, our digital twins are the fruits of our own labor. We invest significant time and energy into our profiles. We make decisions about which pictures to upload, with whom to share information, and what to comment on the posts of others. Creating a digital twin is a creative act. And if our energy went into creating it, it belongs to us.

The fact that we use discretion doesn't make it any less our own property, or any less an extension of us; in fact, choosing how to express ourselves is perhaps the most intimate extension of our own identity. Just because an artist uses commercial paint (as opposed to making his own), that doesn't mean that the paint company owns his work. He made decisions on how to use that paint, and those decisions are an extremely personal reflection of his own vision and identity. Why shouldn't the ownership of digital selves stay with the creator, just like the ownership of a painting stays with the painter?

Creations of Your Mind on Blockchain: Rethinking the Ownership

With the growth in digital music and, more recently, music streaming, the music industry will have to consider new ways of remunerating artists and valuing creativity. Remember Taylor Swift's war with Spotify? Could blockchain have been the solution?

Entrepreneurs are increasingly turning to blockchain to make content sharing fairer for artists. Several companies are capitalizing on smart contracts to allow revenue on purchases of creative work to be automatically disseminated based on licensing agreements, according to CB Insights.

You can't discuss digital rights and music without mentioning the future of streaming services. Here's just one. Last year, Spotify acquired Mediachain, a digital rights management start-up. Mediachain has been working on using blockchain technology to solve problems with attribution—an area where Spotify needs help. Online tech industry publication TechCrunch noted that it had to settle a lawsuit over unpaid royalties.[3]

---

[3]V. Gupta. Discussions with the author. 2019.F. Arisandi. 2018. "Mattereum Is Unlike Any Blockchain Projects You've Ever Heard of." https://www.chepicap.com/en/news/5110/mattereum-is-not-the-like-any-of-blockchain-projects-you-ve-ever-heard-of.html. More information about Mattereum is available at https://mattereum.com/. More information about JAAK is available at https://jaak.io/.K. Jackson. Discussions with the author. 2019.More information about Ujo Music is available at https://www.ujomusic.com. More information about Audius is available at https://audius.co/. More information about Open Music is available at http://open-music.org/. EY Global Leader. 2016. "Blockchain Reaction Tech Companies Plan for Critical Mass." https://www.ey.com/Publication/vwLUAssets/ey-blockchain-reaction-tech-companies-plan-for-critical-mass/$FILE/ey-blockchain-reaction.pdf. S. Perez. 2017. "Spotify Acquires Blockchain Startup Mediachain to Solve Music's Attribution Problem." https://techcrunch.com/2017/04/26/spotify-acquires-blockchain-startup-mediachain-to-solve-musics-attribution-problem/.

Eliminating Digital Rights Theft

Blockchain could effectively eliminate digital rights theft. It could enable artists to release their music and control the data and terms of use on their own terms, and royalties would be distributed in real time via smart contracts. "If anytime anybody uses a music file anywhere in the world, that action is automatically recorded by a public blockchain, and the transaction would be validated. You'd have no digital rights theft," explains Greg Cudahy, EY Global Leader, writing in "Blockchain reaction: Tech plans for critical mass."[4]

The Open Music Initiative[5] is a consortium that seeks to leverage blockchain technology to resolve royalty disputes. It's not building a platform. Instead, it's creating an open-source protocol for the uniform identification of music rights holders and creators. Likewise, other companies such as Audius[6] that aims to eliminate middlemen in the music sector and

---

[4]V. Gupta. Discussions with the author. 2019.F. Arisandi. 2018. "Mattereum Is Unlike Any Blockchain Projects You've Ever Heard of." https://www.chepicap.com/en/news/5110/mattereum-is-not-the-like-any-of-blockchain-projects-you-ve-ever-heard-of.html. More information about Mattereum is available at https://mattereum.com/. More information about JAAK is available at https://jaak.io/.K. Jackson. Discussions with the author. 2019.More information about Ujo Music is available at https://www.ujomusic.com. More information about Audius is available at https://audius.co/. More information about Open Music is available at http://open-music.org/. EY Global Leader. 2016. "Blockchain Reaction Tech Companies Plan for Critical Mass." https://www.ey.com/Publication/vwLUAssets/ey-blockchain-reaction-tech-companies-plan-for-critical-mass/$FILE/ey-blockchain-reaction.pdf.

[5]V. Gupta. Discussions with the author. 2019.F. Arisandi. 2018. "Mattereum Is Unlike Any Blockchain Projects You've Ever Heard of." https://www.chepicap.com/en/news/5110/mattereum-is-not-the-like-any-of-blockchain-projects-you-ve-ever-heard-of.html. More information about Mattereum is available at https://mattereum.com/. More information about JAAK is available at https://jaak.io/.K. Jackson. Discussions with the author. 2019.More information about Ujo Music is available at https://www.ujomusic.com. More information about Audius is available at https://audius.co/. More information about Open Music is available at http://open-music.org/.

[6]V. Gupta. Discussions with the author. 2019.F. Arisandi. 2018. "Mattereum Is Unlike Any Blockchain Projects You've Ever Heard of." https://www.chepicap.com/en/news/5110/mattereum-is-not-the-like-any-of-blockchain-projects-you-ve-ever-heard-of.html. More information about Mattereum is available at https://mattereum

Ujo Music[7] that aims to change the way things were remixed will likely disrupt the music industry soon.

Content Creators Suffer the Most

Founded in 2016, SingularDTV launched its content-driven blockchain-powered entertainment dApp Breaker in January 2019. During our discussion, Breaker's co-founder and CEO Kim Jackson[8] emphasized that transparent value exchange, the main component of blockchain, helps artists retain more control over their creations. She says, "It could ensure total control over rights, revenue, and royalties, and a direct relationship between artists and fans."

Jackson explains,

> As an entertainment executive I was very aware of the issues that independent film companies face. It's tough to sustain a business model that does not allow you to retain value because intermediates such as Netflix and Amazon extract value. And currently that's the main way you can get your intellectual property (IP) distributed to mass audiences.

.com/. More information about JAAK is available at https://jaak.io/.K. Jackson. Discussions with the author. 2019.More information about Ujo Music is available at https://www.ujomusic.com. More information about Audius is available at https://audius.co/.

[7]V. Gupta. Discussions with the author. 2019.F. Arisandi. 2018. "Mattereum Is Unlike Any Blockchain Projects You've Ever Heard of." https://www.chepicap.com/en/news/5110/mattereum-is-not-the-like-any-of-blockchain-projects-you-ve-ever-heard-of.html. More information about Mattereum is available at https://mattereum.com/. More information about JAAK is available at https://jaak.io/.K. Jackson. Discussions with the author. 2019.More information about Ujo Music is available at https://www.ujomusic.com.

[8]V. Gupta. Discussions with the author. 2019.F. Arisandi. 2018. "Mattereum Is Unlike Any Blockchain Projects You've Ever Heard of." https://www.chepicap.com/en/news/5110/mattereum-is-not-the-like-any-of-blockchain-projects-you-ve-ever-heard-of.html. More information about Mattereum is available at https://mattereum.com/. More information about JAAK is available at https://jaak.io/.K. Jackson. Discussions with the author. 2019.

Jackson noted,

> If you're a content creator, and you sell your content, you're out of that equation. There's no sustainable business model for continued revenue because the creator is cut off from the data related to the audience behavior and revenue reporting. You are also decoupled from IP because you signed away your rights for, say, 15 years. There was a problem in our business models from independent content creators' perspective; we are learning intrinsically what blockchain technology could provide.

Producer and artist Gramatik, as featured in Alex Winter's Trust Machine: The Story of Blockchain, a Breaker original production. Copyright: Breaker.

Putting the Creator at the Center with Data

Jackson and her co-founder Zach LeBeau were joined by Ethereum co-founder Joseph Lubin in creating SingularDTV. According to Jackson,

> For me it was always about the distribution platform tool, where content creators can track and monetize their IP. Consider a film. I knew I would be able to see where people were watching it. As a content creator, you would be able to collect data on your audience and, most importantly, own the data and benefit firsthand from the revenue.

Such a model allows for content creators to stay in control of their business model.

The business model now is still one-sided. You could raise money and create content, but it's doubtful that you're going to be able to see a return on that content. Your investors are not going to see their return. Most importantly, you can't even provide them with any transparent accounting to show them that there was an activity because you have been completely cut off from it. Essentially, what we saw was an opportunity to build a distribution platform for content creators that operated the same way. We know through market research that audiences don't care where they find content, be it a movie or a piece of music—they want ease. They want it when they want it, where they want it. They don't care if it's on iTunes, Netflix, HBO. They want the show.

Breaker has created something that, according to Jackson, addresses the needs of both the audience and the content creators.

From the audience perspective, we built something that operated the same as what they are used to. But from a content creator perspective, it is different because you, as a content creator, are the one who gets to benefit, and now you can create a business model based on it. Whether you're an individual artist, a production company, or especially a studio with large accounting overhead, you're able to have this peer-to-peer transparent accounting, IP tracking, and data collection, and you own it. That is powerful; it is one of our business models, and that is what we are building. We are still a start-up. We've been in business for about 2 years now, and we only launched our beta product to the world in January. Now that we are in beta, we're testing how people interact with it.

Never mind leading the audience into new solutions, just keeping up with audience preferences in a fast-paced world isn't always straightforward.

Breaker is available as a desktop and a mobile app. People want it on their phone, or they want to listen to music on their phone, or they want to watch something at home on another device. We're building that. In the meantime, we have produced original content, and we've acquired some more content so that we can test and learn how our product operates. We needed to own content that was ours so that we could experiment with how we want it to perform, as well as to test new models. You prove how they will work and how they will benefit in the marketplace. You can turn around and market it properly to both content creators and audiences.

Do audiences care about the nature of their relationship with the artist? According to Jackson, "We are learning whether we can get audiences to care about that relationship. Do they care whether their money is going directly into the artist's pockets or is used to 'paying the man?' How do we get them to care about a local exchange and a peer-to-peer exchange? Out of the gate, the data and the marketing say they don't care. They want to come home, get a glass of wine, and watch what they want to watch, and they don't want more steps. They don't want to work for their entertainment."

"We're looking at film, television, music, eBooks, any IP," continues Jackson.

Essentially, any IP can have a channel with under-the-hood functionality. Hopefully, in the future, we can allow people to participate in the success of an entertainment endeavor and an artist. That's the long-term vision. It is tied to the whole token economy, and with that, there are regulations and complexities. It isn't easy. Right now, we're focused on film, though we will be going into music soon. It's a big opportunity. It is a slightly different business model and a huge nut to crack. We're talking about releasing the song and the movie at the same time.

Putting Creator at the Center with Payments

In terms of payment, an understanding of audience needs goes a long way in making a platform user-friendly.

You don't have to use crypto; you can also use a credit card. We gave users that option on purpose. We didn't want the regular audience to be freaked out by having to use new technology. Although you can, and we do show people how to make a wallet. I always encourage it.

What is Jackson's long-term vision for Breaker?

The vision is a lofty set of decentralized entertainment platform tools. I would be so thrilled to see that become a reality. But there are a lot of steps and a lot of obstacles before then. That's the purest vision, and we are purist in that sense, but it gets tough because we do have to make compromises.

Considering its potential for the entertainment media industry, we can see that blockchain could address problems from content access, distribution, and compensation to managing assets, digital rights, and financing. There are other examples too. British blockchain start-up JAAK[9] is developing an Ethereum-based platform that allows media owners to convert their repository of media, metadata, and rights into "smart content" that can self-execute licensing transactions (CB Insights). It is building a blockchain platform "to bring clear and timely payments to the creative class." They allow creatives to publish content, manage contracts, and transact payments from a single portal.

Property, Commodities, and Real Property: New Flavors of Ownership

Digitizing Physical Objects and Real Assets

If we are going to put ourselves and creations of our minds on blockchain, why not digitize and put real, physical objects on blockchain as well? It is a logical next step, to the extent one finds digitizing physical objects logical. Real-world assets can be put on blockchain by separating asset ownership into its constituent parts.

Of course, digitizing physical assets is not a new concept. If you have ever scanned a document, you have created a digital copy of it and

---

[9]V. Gupta. Discussions with the author. 2019.F. Arisandi. 2018. "Mattereum Is Unlike Any Blockchain Projects You've Ever Heard of." https://www.chepicap.com/en/news/5110/mattereum-is-not-the-like-any-of-blockchain-projects-you-ve-ever-heard-of.html. More information about Mattereum is available at https://mattereum.com/. More information about JAAK is available at https://jaak.io/.

digitized it. In fact, do you remember when Google Books began scanning all 130 million distinct titles in the world? Do you remember how controversial that was? It is not hard to imagine that we will see a similar controversy when it comes to digitizing physical objects and real property.

For example, the team behind Mattereum[10] is intrigued by the idea of achieving legal title over every physical object in the world using blockchain technology as the medium. The team is trying to "bridge the gap between programmable blockchain smart contracts and actual legal contracts." The underlying legal concept is that all assets have owners who can decide how best to manage them.[11]

When registrars on Mattereum network are granted legal title over certain assets, they can set up on-chain smart contracts through which assets can be programmatically purchased, sold, rented, assigned, and partitioned. The granted legal title will be used to resolve disputes and enforce resolutions as well.

Vinay Gupta,[12] CEO of Mattereum, observes,

> I think a lot of this is just legal spaces beginning to acquire concepts from software engineering. And some of those concepts will come across as foreign. Both computer programmers and lawyers deal with large texts. But computer programmers have 50 different tools for helping them manage text. And lawyers just have one tool—Microsoft Word.

Lawyers Are Programmers Who Made a Wrong Career Choice

Gupta wonders,

---

[10]V. Gupta. Discussions with the author. 2019.F. Arisandi. 2018. "Mattereum Is Unlike Any Blockchain Projects You've Ever Heard of." https://www.chepicap.com/en/news/5110/mattereum-is-not-the-like-any-of-blockchain-projects-you-ve-ever-heard-of .html. More information about Mattereum is available at https://mattereum.com/.

[11]V. Gupta. Discussions with the author. 2019.F. Arisandi. 2018. "Mattereum Is Unlike Any Blockchain Projects You've Ever Heard of." https://www.chepicap.com/en/news/5110/mattereum-is-not-the-like-any-of-blockchain-projects-you-ve-ever-heard-of.html.

[12]V. Gupta. Discussions with the author. 2019.

Why don't lawyers have more sophisticated tools for managing texts? Why don't they have the same kind of tools that programmers use for managing texts at large scale? There are tools for simple things like finding the location of content, comparing it to another document, and seeing who touched it last. But why is that stuff not substantially automated in legal practice!?

In Discussing Mattereum, Gupta explains, "At a high level, we are building a tool to change the legal ownership of an object. We want to be able to change the ownership of the objects by putting money into a contract." He continues,

> There are multiple classes of property: serialized unique objects like a Stradivarius violin, and registered objects, like houses, cars, and boats, which live on a government register. The same object can be both. For example, cars are both serialized and registered property. In fact, almost everything that is registered is serialized as well. The idea is that you take this object and put it in a smart contract. The goal is to have the owner in smart contracts make changes in the real world to legally transfer ownership.

So back to the Stradivarius violin. If its legal title was assigned to one of Mattereum's registrars, the violin would be not just a physical asset but a digital asset as well. Then it could be programmatically tokenized and sold to multiple investors. Thus, the contractual restrictions regarding its use could be required and enforced. Rather than staying locked away in a vault, it could be used to bring joy to the ears of many, with Mattereum managing how many times it's played each year and where.

The same principle applies to artists who want to sell their work to consortiums of investors. They then can manage whether their art will be displayed in public galleries the whole year, the income percentages received by all involved parties, and so on.

Enhancing Value by Recording an Object's Milestones

Blockchain is very good at managing truth. We set up different mechanisms depending on the value of the goods, the jurisdiction, and what you want to do with them. Gupta adds, "We pull together the supporting documentation around a certain Stradivarius violin, such as X-rays, historical documents, maintenance records, performer notes, and other stuff. We pull that together into basically a digital portfolio of this object. Each piece of data is used for an authenticity indemnity."

Gupta explains,

> This way, you have built-in damages. Specifically, a built-in consequential loss indemnity that is also an elegant representation of actionable thoughts about the objects. Ideally, we want every object to be sold through an insurance vending machine type of process—buyers can simply pay for authentication cover as they purchase. In doing so, we are creating that record that also enhances the value of the violin.

So what else can you do with a Mattereum platform? "We're very interested in doing climate work on the back of this," Gupta explains. He continues, "For example, each object can contain emissions data associated with it. In other words, we're in a position of pushing morality using our platform."

Formalizing Informal Insurance All Around Us

Gupta explains,

> Insurance is critical to commercial transactions. In the real world, everything is interconnected. Everything is also a bit difficult and unpredictable. Rather than having to deal with a messy dispute resolution, we want these insurance policies in place so that if you've got, say, a 1 percent defect rate because the world is a little flaky, you spread that 1 percent across all the customers. And when something goes wrong, you just pull from that pool. It is a really simple and straightforward approach like the one used by credit card companies today.

> The world is filled with informal insurance. For example, the guy at the hotel who upgrades your room because your room has a bad radiator. That is a mini insurance scheme. He's got a pool of resources to make decisions. And those little buffers are all over

the physical world. There are many of these little schemes where you've got a small pool of resources informally controlled. They are handed out to cover the kind of errors in the material world. It's not that somebody has the discretion to upgrade your room, give you a better table, pour you a free cup of coffee. We are formalizing these systems so you can make them efficient. But it's formalized and automated.

Conclusion

Among the trickiest, and most exciting, challenges that the explosive development of blockchain technology faces relates to ownership. The questions begin with simpler ones: who owns what exists on the blockchain; some normative questions like who *should* own what exists on the blockchain? But when we think expansively, we can see that it's not just our own selves being tokenized for security and efficiency but our actions and transactions as well. When a creator is closer to the object of their creation, they maintain control and cut out the inefficiencies of the proverbial "middleman." From lawyers, to artists, to asset managers, a range of actors in the global economy stand to gain from the new conceptions of ownership possible with blockchain.

CHAPTER 5

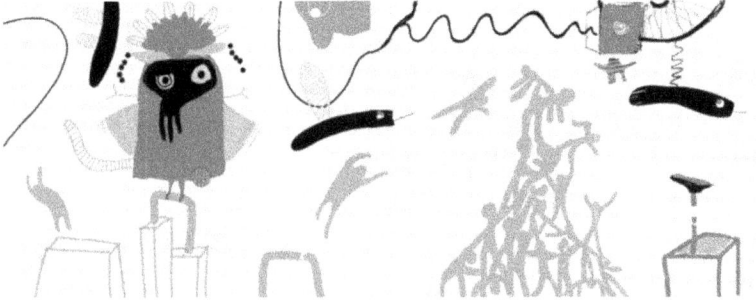

DADA Collective: Isa Kost, Italy / Mar Espi, Spain, collaboratively created using blockchain technology, a visual conversation.

The Power of Teamwork: How Blockchain Can Change the Virtual World through Collaboration and Open-Source Software

DADA Collective: Otro Captore, Chile / Beatriz Ramos, USA, collaboratively created using blockchain technology, a visual conversation, a visual conversation.

What would the world look like if John Lennon and Paul McCartney never met? If Larry Page and Sergey Brin never teamed up to transform the Internet? What if William Procter and James Gamble, Ben Cohen and Jerry Greenfield, or (my favorite example of fashionable shoes!) Jimmy Choo and Tamara Mellon never joined forces? The world would be very different for sure.

History is full of powerful collaborations on micro and macro scales. Why? The results of such collaborations can be greater than the sum of their parts because bringing together different talents, perspectives, and fields enables us to create something more than we ever could on our own.

Often, the results of collaborations are even better than hoped. Sometimes, collaboration lets us overcome obstacles we never thought we could. Other times, collaboration allows us to find a novel solution, be daring, and address long-standing problems. And best of all, in the process, we can learn from others and make a huge impact.

Blockchain can enable a different and deeper collaboration by tapping into the power of underutilized resources like hobbyists, local communities, the power of impact, connecting the virtual and real worlds, and new open-source development. In other words, "If you want to go fast, go alone. If you want to go far, go together." Blockchain technology can help us go far. Much, much farther than we thought was possible.

Blockchain technology enables radical collaboration.

Leveraging the Power of Amateurs and Hobbyists

In 2005, Jeff Howe and Mark Robinson, editors at Wired, coined the term "crowdsourcing" to describe how businesses were using the Internet to "outsource work to the crowd." In *The Rise of Crowdsourcing*, in June 2006, Howe first published a definition for the term:

> Simply defined, crowdsourcing represents the act of a company or institution taking a function once performed by employees and outsourcing it to an undefined (and generally large) network of people in the form of an open call. This can take the form of peer-production (when the job is performed collaboratively) but is also often undertaken by sole individuals. The crucial prerequisite is the use of the open call format and the large network of potential laborers.

Since then, we have seen many variations and implementations of crowdsourcing. Because blockchain technology is so good at keeping records in chronological order, it can enable even greater collaborations. For example, it can help bring together amateur hobbyists to lead progress across fields.

Meet GlobalXplorer,[1] a nonprofit crowdsourced platform to analyze the incredible wealth of satellite images currently available to archaeologists. It is the brainchild of Sarah Parcak, 2016 TED Prize winner[2] and National Geographic Fellow, who has attracted attention for using technology to locate ancient sites.

The goal of GlobalXplorer is to democratize the wonder of archaeological discovery and help us connect to the past. Relying on satellite technology, Dr. Parcak is creating a global network of citizen explorers and revolutionizing the field of archaeology. Anyone with Internet can discover hidden civilizations or locate sites where looting has taken place.

---

[1]More information about GlobalXplorer is available at https://www.globalxplorer.org/.
[2]K.T. May. 2019. "Calling All GlobalXplorers: Get Ready to Go to India." https://blog.ted.com/calling-all-globalxplorers-get-ready-to-go-to-india/. See also K. Killgrove. 2017. "Space Archaeologist Funds Citizen Science Platform with $1M TED Prize." https://www.forbes.com/sites/kristinakillgrove/2017/01/30/space-archaeologist-funds-citizen-science-platform-with-1m-ted-prize/#33e600a73bed.

To develop trusted ways to verify an object's provenance—to protect museums and other purchasers from buying looted objects—GlobalXplorer joined ConsenSys Ventures' Tachyon program in 2018. Together, they will use Ethereum-based blockchain technology to develop a centralized repository and marketplace for anyone working with ancient artifacts and archaeological sites and track objects from when they are discovered to when they go on display in museums. Ideally, this collaboration will combat looting and the illegal purchase of antiquities. Along the way, it will help museums monetize their collections.[3]

The Rise of Local Communities and Economies

Collaborations can be hyperlocal for the benefit of a specific community to solve a specific problem. For example, BULVRD[4] is a global mapping community in which you can earn cryptocurrency for making road reports and driving. After you install the BULVRD Drive app and start driving, you receive real-time road reports, such as traffic, police, and hazards. It gives you traffic-aware turn-by-turn navigation to ensure you arrive at your destination on time.

When you drive using BULVRD, you earn tokens. You can drop tokens along a route to incentivize driving certain routes and influence the development of future reports. If you develop road reports like traffic and hazards, you earn more tokens. You can then "drop" your tokens on your routes to encourage other drivers to report to be able to find the quickest way. Or a business can drop tokens in front of their stores, or a user can drop tokens on various routes to find the quickest way!

---

[3]S. Rebman. 2018. "Birmingham Organization Tapped for Global Blockchain Accelerator Program." https://www.bizjournals.com/birmingham/news/2018/09/18/birmingham-organization-tapped-for-global.html. GlobalXplorer. 2018. "GlobalXplorer's Blockchain for Antiquities Joins Tachyon Accelerator, Consensys Ventures' New Flagship Initiative." https://medium.com/@globalxplorer/globalxplorer-s-blockchain-for-antiquities-joins-tachyon-accelerator-consensys-ventures-new-fab4ee118fa0; D. Pena. 2018. "GlobalXplorer Selected For Blockchain Accelerator Program." https://cryptoblockwire.com/globalxplorer-gets-a-valuable-chance/.
[4]More information about BULVRD is available at https://bulvrdapp.com/.

On the back-end, BULVRD leverages the Ethereum blockchain with smart contracts to manage rewards and create new datasets. Using non-fungible tokens or NFTs (digital collectibles), you can stake your digital collectible on the map to show to the world or use it as a new marketing avenue when selling it. You can also earn custom BULVRD digital collectibles for your contributions in the ecosystem. Finally, it also leverages geospatial augmented reality experiences to give community members a new way to interact with the world around them, including automation via machine learning and artificial intelligence.

Unleashing Creative Collaboration and Co-creation across the World

That same blockchain technology may facilitate unprecedented collaboration across borders. For example, Beatriz Helena Ramos,[5] founder of Dada, a social network where people speak to each other through digital drawings creating collaborative art, explains,

> We are creating a whole economy using blockchain. I'm an artist. But I don't come from the art world. I come from the entertainment industry. I worked many years in animation, and my first job was at MTV as a painter. I worked for Disney. Then I opened my own animation studio with a contract to work for *Teenage Mutant Ninja Turtles*. I directed over a hundred commercials for some of the biggest brands in the world such as Coca Cola. But here's the thing, I don't own any of the intellectual rights to the work I've done for 20 years.

According to Ramos,

> The global animation market is worth $300 billion. To put that figure in perspective, the global art market is only $60 billion. Animation is one of those industries where you can easily see who is creating value. The artists are animators, illustrators, writers, musicians, voice-over actors, and designers. It's not that artists don't create value; the problem is that we don't capture any of it.

---

[5]B.H. Ramos. Discussions with the author. 2019.

This is where blockchain comes in. Ramos explains,

We have built a tool for millions of people around the world to make and access digital art. Using blockchain, we can now guarantee that artists have full control of their work and that the value they create stays within the community."

Nonfungible tokens allow for digital artworks to be probably unique, therefore allowing it to capture value. It also provides intellectual property protection and proof of ownership.

Dada allows you to create visual conversations. It's all created on the platform with our tools. Someone makes a drawing, you reply to it, then others reply to it, and magic happens. Ramos observes, "The beautiful part is that all of this has been created by different people at different times in different countries who have never met each other. It's a completely spontaneous process and is a new way of making art."

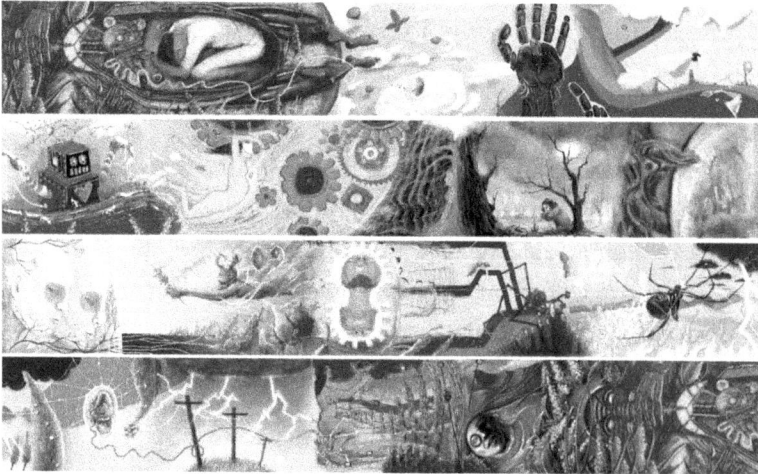

Soul In The Machine: Visual conversation collaboratively created using blockchain technology made by 19 artists from 12 countries and live-streamed at the Ethereal Summit in New York, June 2019. https://soulinthemachine.dada.nyc/.

"We have thousands of these visual conversations. Dada currently holds the largest collection of tokenized digital art. We have a hundred thousand drawings ready to be traded as NFTs." These NFTs can be layered into one single image that someone can own. Ramos continues,

Pase Mágico: Visual conversation collaboratively created using blockchain technology by Otro Captore, Beatriz Helena Ramos, Boris Toledo Doorm and Talita Sotomayor.

We can now build the tools for anyone to use these drawings and add value on top of them, they'll be able to animate them, and add text or music to these visual conversations. If there is a commercial value to what's created, every contributor will receive their fair share.

Ramos explains,

I can easily see how a visual conversation may become a book, and where the artists and the collectors share the profits of the sales. I can also see how animators could come in spontaneously and give life to characters. We could make it into a property that could generate thousands, even hundreds of thousands of dollars in revenues. All the value staying within the community.

In this new model, artists can make art for the sole enjoyment of it without any pressure to produce. Collective ownership and shared profits will allow artists to live full and rewarding lives while at the same time contributing their value to the community.

A new economic paradigm for a self-governed community is that it owns the value it creates and directly controls the means of production, distribution, and profit-sharing of its collective work. In this system, artists will receive a guaranteed basic income for their contribution, allowing them to do what they love and make art freely.

Proliferating the Impact and Acts of Kindness

If blockchain can harness artistic thinking from all over the world to change how we create, and even what creative processes look like, how can we use blockchain for impact?

Meet Plastic Bank.[6] Its goal is simple: to stop pollution of the ocean with plastic by making it more valuable. To do this, it transforms plastic waste into currency by empowering the most impoverished people in the world to convert the pollution in their communities into wealth.

Shaun Frankson,[7] co-founder and CTO of Plastic Bank observes,

> We started looking at how to stop ocean plastic. How do we not treat our ocean as garbage disposal? If you walk into a kitchen sink that is overflowing with water, what would you do first? The answer is obvious: you'd turn it off. We started to look at how we do that.

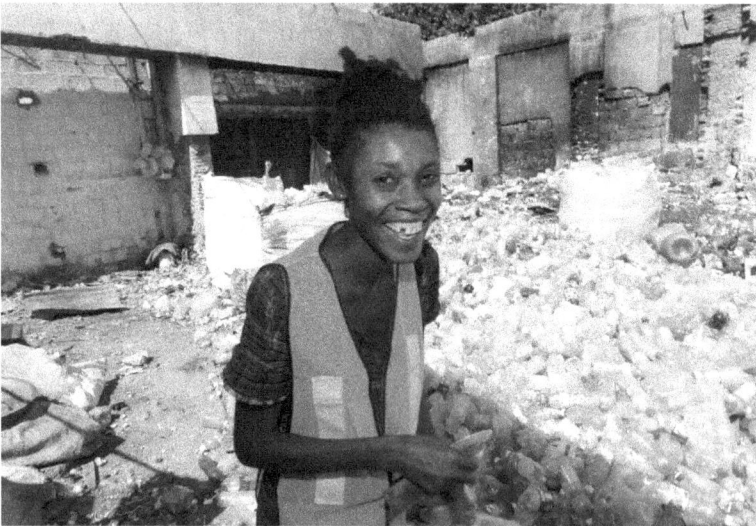

---

[6]More information about Plastic Bank is available at https://www.plasticbank.com/.
[7]S. Frankson. Discussions with the author. 2019.

He observes,

The problem of ocean plastic starts with developing countries with no waste management system. In fact, it is a common practice for people in developing countries to push the garbage into the streets, which then ends up in the waterways. When you throw something away, it must go somewhere. All too often, it's the ocean.

Asia is one of the biggest contributors to ocean plastic. Many countries around the continent have almost no waste management systems and abundant poverty. Frankson says,

They are also sitting on acres of diamonds and they don't realize it. Did you know that the pound-for-pound value of plastic when sorted is more than that of steel? How do you pair this opportunity with this abundance of plastic to start capturing the value of plastic?

Frankson continues,

What's the threshold cost for plastic to not end up in the ocean? A dollar? No it's really a matter of pennies. And this is where we started to look at how we can change the perception of plastic to harness this opportunity.

It turns out that around the world there are many people called waste pickers and scavengers who collect plastic.

Plastic Banks is transforming this industry to dignify recycling while creating a global revolution around social plastic. Frankson explains,

Our business premise is to make plastic too valuable to end up in the ocean. We realized that 300 g of plastic has a market value of about $0.10. If the same 300 g of plastic is changed into the shape of a phone case, you suddenly have a $20 to $30 item. If you think about it, just the change in the shape of plastic turns waste into value.

How do you reveal value in plastic? About 80 percent of plastic comes from developing countries, mostly in Southeast Asia. Ironically, these impoverished nations treat plastic as garbage. They fail to see that if plastic is collected, sorted, and recycled, the pound of plastic is valuable. It's an amazing opportunity. Plastic Bank was born to dignify recycling and empower communities to take plastic resources that are lying around and use it to create value.

Frankson says, "We came to realize that when you treat people as a supply chain, it is a very cold world. The world begins to change when you build a supply chain that puts people first." He continued, "We wanted to give pride and dignity to recycling where we can stabilize the price."

Plastic Bank brings value to plastic. People pick up the plastic and bring it to a plastic bank. Each location operates as an independent local cooperative. The plastic is sorted by type, color, and weight. Then a value is attached to that weight. In certified locations, a special digital bonus payment is earned on top of the market rate of plastic. This ensures collectors can provide for their families and send their children to school. According to Frankson, all plastic from this program is turned into social plastic. It is used by large companies to package their product instead of new plastic.

Frankson explains,

> We realized that the entire model of recycling needs to be ethical, sustainable, stable, and dignified. Where it would never go below a certain floor because of market conditions. And that's really where our social plastic came from. How can we stabilize the price and continuously increase the value of plastic for both collectors and communities?

Plastic Bank is built on Hyperledger Fabric in the IBM cloud. Frankson says,

> I'm an advocate for blockchain for business and using smart contracts for just about every condition of what can and can't happen with the system. I support having blockchain be the trusted data and smart contracts being trusted with decision-making. You can get instant, real-time, unlimited scale of any exchange of assets. This is especially critical for us as we are an exchange-based system.

He explains,

> When someone goes to a plastic bank to exchange plastic for value of some kind, we track everything using smart contracts. Whether it's an exchange of cash for plastic, an exchange for goods and services within these markets, or an exchange for our digital reward tokens. Blockchain and smart contracts allow these exchanges to happen.

Frankson explains, "Data recording is done by smart contracts, and identification is done in blockchain code. We store data in blockchain code and the decision-making capabilities for just about anything to do with it."

He continues,

> Our business model is always evolving. We continue to tweak the business model and work in different cultures, different climates, with different income levels, and in different geographies. We are increasingly able to go straight to the household and businesses, which is very exciting. We think it is an opportunity for impact.

Recently Plastic Bank partnered with SC Johnson where they sponsored development in Indonesia. Frankson explained,

> There we have an active full digital ecosystem. So, someone could receive secure digital savings through our program. They can spend those digital savings at the local markets. If I'm a collector, I have a digital identity, I have a digital wallet, and I can find where to bring my plastic and where to get the digital rewards. If I'm a store owner, I can run a point-of-sale system and an inventory system and again having a digital wallet where if someone wants to buy my goods. All of this is enabled by blockchain.

Blockchain plays a big part in how Plastic Bank can do this. Frankson explains,

> For us, blockchain is the trust stamp. It's how we can provide a trusted transparent supply chain. It's how we can provide financial inclusion. It's how we can establish a private identity for some of the most vulnerable people on the planet. Blockchain is delivering on our promise of doing good. Blockchain is a powerful tool and is amazing.

Connecting Real World and Third Place

Most people live between two social environments: home ("first place") and the workplace ("second place"). Yet for many of us that's not all. We have a "third place," social surroundings separate from the home and workplace. These places could be churches, cafes, clubs, public libraries, or parks—or anywhere else we spend time outside of home or work.

Have you ever noticed that you seem to be spending more and more time online? My children live in their video game worlds. They have full lives and identities there. In fact, for many of us, social apps and video games have effectively become the third place where we go to socialize, debate, and have fun.

Ray Oldenburg argues in his influential book *The Great Good Place* that third places are essential to civil society, democracy, and civic engagement. They establish feelings of a sense of place that we don't get elsewhere. They also help establish a feeling of belonging. Could blockchain technology help us create third places online—virtual churches, cafes, clubs, public libraries, or parks—that can hold our rupturing society together? Why not? As a form of technology, it is just another form of collaboration that prioritizes belonging and community.

Other scholars have summed up Oldenburg's view of the third place in eight characteristics. Among those are that they tend to be a neutral ground with no obligation to join. They also tend to be a leveling space where your economic or social status does not matter, and anyone can participate equally and freely. The main activity revolves around happy and playful conversation. Accessibility and accommodation, the presence of "regulars," and keeping a low profile and playful mood are some of the norms. A third place is a home away from home where you feel warmth, possession, and belonging.

Decentraland is an example of a third place.[8] It is an open-source initiative to build a virtual world that runs on open standards and uses Ethereum blockchain technology to track ownership. It is made up of 90,000 pulses of lumber, or 10-m squares. There, you can trade, develop, and monetize the virtual land by building on top of it. MANA is Decentraland's currency and can be used to purchase land and make in-game purchases. If you own land in Decentraland, you can build and monetize your games, artistic experiences, or social applications. At Decentraland, you can create, experience, and monetize immersive 3D, interactive global content and applications.

The land in Decentraland has been distributed in many ways. For example, you can pay thousands of dollars in cryptocurrency to participate and build whatever you can dream of on your virtual land. Maybe, you can even turn a profit one day! While there is debate around whether this investment will have an upside, Decentraland is a risky investment. Some have paid more than $28 million for blocks, which is the largest ever sale of virtual land.

Although it is hard to predict the future success of Decentraland, you can be sure that it will correlate with whether there are good games that entice participants. Themed neighborhoods, festival land, Vegas City, games, universities, and other establishments are currently being built. And best of all, once you have built something, no one can knock down your creation. And unlike other virtual worlds in which companies operate centrally, control all land, and store all the content on their servers, Decentraland's developers plan to eventually withdraw from operating the platform.

This is where the blockchain technology is critical. The plot owners will run Decentraland. Presumably, this reduces the risk of a central company's arbitrary, capricious decisions (e.g., sudden rule change) or going out of business.

To some extent, Decentraland promises to deliver a virtual version of a libertarian utopian society. No one can remove your user content at Decentraland, not even a government. Of course, users can favor some content and filter out others. There are also community-based filters. After

---

[8]More information about Decentraland is available at https://decentraland.org/.

all, presumably, plot owners are motivated to make money. Perhaps they will make prudent content decisions for their communities.

Open-Source: Innovation on Steroids

Though the sharing of technical information predates the advent of the Internet and the personal computer, it is undeniable that the open software movement has been critical to the proliferation of the Internet and its applications. The main principle of open-source software development is peer-production, with products such as source code, blueprints, and documentation freely available and accessible to the public. Many large formal institutions have supported the development of the open-source movement.

Though open source creates huge value, some classify it as an infor-good or knowledge which involves significant investment to create, but the cost of reproducing is, or is near, zero. Thereby lies the challenge of incentivizing the production of high-quality open-source code.

Keving Owocki, the founder of Gitcoin, observes in one of the interviews,

> Almost all applications in the world rely on open-source software. The vast majority are built on the shoulders of giants, people who've done open source in the past. All these brands that you're familiar with and you interact with every day already use open-source software. This is the foundation that modern software infrastructure is built upon. Almost $400 billion of economic value is created by open-source software. While the blockchain system is truly massive, the wider open-source ecosystem is even bigger.[9]

Remember NFT ERC-721 tokens from Chapter 3? They are much more than CryptoKitties (as cute as they are). They can be useful. NFTs are almost like badges, trophies, or kudos. They can represent actions or accomplishments like gold stars your elementary school gave you every time you turned in your homework on time, or loyalty points from your favorite store, hotel, or airline.

---

[9]https://www.youtube.com/watch?v=PKujxIfRmfI.

It turns out that a digital trophy case is very useful for fostering collaboration. What if you could earn tokens or badges for completing requests to make open-source contributions? What if you eventually could convert your collection of badges into a degree or some sort of accreditation to signal expertise? What if you could convert your collection of badges into a reward?

In other words, NFTs can be used to encourage certain socially desirable actions in various networks and communities. In this case, they can be used to encourage contribution to open source.

According to Ian Lapham,[10] a blockchain engineer, "We need to change your perspective on how you view NFTs. When we look at NFTs at face value, we think of CryptoKitties, A game." Lapham explains that secondary use cases make NFTs valuable. He continues, "It's important to start thinking of NFTs in other ways. NFTs are almost like badges or trophies or just general representations of actions or accomplishments you've made within a network such as voting on governance."

Lapham explains,

> There are really no incentives to vote on any proposals. If you're awarded an NFT representing that you voted on this item, then maybe some third-party developer can see that you voted on it and will want to incentivize you to do other things. Then your vote becomes an actual asset. It is now a digital good.

According to Lapham, viewing NFTs in a new light can unleash creativity in new products and services. Lapham says, "It becomes more powerful when we start thinking about the interactions and the bundles of actions that we can take with collections of NFTs. You can start to get creative with it and think of some interesting use cases."

Lapham explains how NFTs can lead to a renaissance in open source. According to him,

> The idea is that if you contribute to open source, you get a form of digital goods, say a badge. They have value and you can exchange it for whatever. It could be tickets, other goods, or money. The money could be in whatever form you like—Ether, Bitcoin, a stable coin, fiat, or something else.

---

[10]I. Lapham. Discussions with the author. 2019.

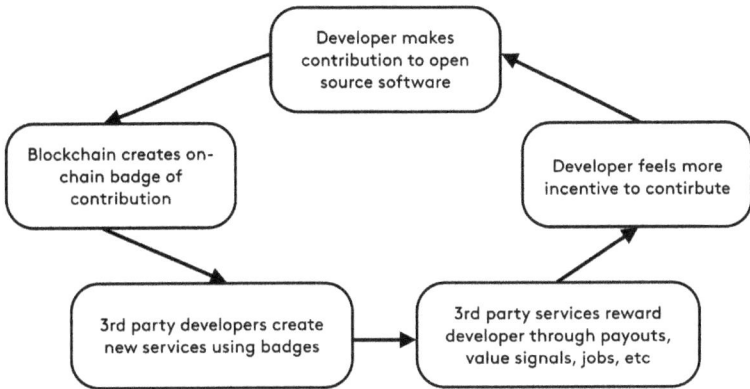

Open source contribution cycle - enhanced through open protocols.

According to Lapham, when you contribute to open source, you are effectively collecting various rewards. This collection may be viewed as a form of payment. In other words, if you contribute to an open-source project, you get some benefits in return. This way I can signal my ability as a developer and improve your reputation, social capital, and employment opportunities. Lapham explains, "Once you start using blockchain to explicitly attach awards through your activity, then it becomes more interesting. This allows you to trade."

A sample profile that showcasing users' contributions and rewards.

Once we put these rewards on blockchain, we formalize these kudos and increase their value and uses. It increases the value of social capital or reputation. In the process, they can incentivize certain behaviors. Lapham observes,

If you can track the person who is contributing to my code, voting on your proposals, and writing actively within the thread online, then you know the person is a really good user. You may want to reward them to encourage further engagement. This may further increase incentives for people to contribute to open-source projects.

Enter the world of Gitcoin,[11] a community for developers to collaborate and monetize their skills while working on open-source projects through bounties. Gitcoin is on a mission to make open-source contribution sustainable by allowing developers to choose projects that fit their portfolio, preferences, and time, as well as to incentivize open-source software development in blockchain. As Gitcoin's website explains, "The weight of maintaining open-source falls on the shoulders of 0.01 percent of developers. This is not sustainable. This is not right."

Kevin Owocki, the head of the Gitcoin project, said in one of his interviews,

The Internet has changed the way we live because it has allowed computers to send information over a network without an intermediary. Blockchain I think does the exact same thing for money or for value; it allows you to send it over a network without an intermediary. If you think about what the Internet did to turn our media into entertainment, I just think that if you project that forward it's possible that what Napster did to record companies, blockchain could do to financial services companies. It could change the way we think about work and invest in financial services. That's the broad thinking about blockchain's potential. My specific niche within that is thinking jobs might look like in that ecosystem.[12]

---

[11]More information about Gitcoin is available at https://gitcoin.co/. See also C. Silver. 2017. "Gitcoin Launches Today, Pushing Open-Source Forward with Cryptocurrency Bounties." https://www.forbes.com/sites/curtissilver/2017/09/25/gitcoin-launches-today-pushing-open-source-forward-with-cryptocurrency-bounties/#5ec816c89853.
[12]"Episode 36: Gitcoin Founder on the Future of Open-source Development [Podcast]." 2018. https://www.disruptordaily.com/episode-36-gitcoin-founder-on-the-future-of-open-source-development-podcast/.

Gitcoin leverages its global, on-demand workforce to help you find expert freelance developers to design, test, code, and build your project teams today. It also allows you to crowdfund for your open-source start-up or project to increase your budget and bring in more developers. As a coder, you get paid in crypto for freelance jobs, building features and solving bug bounties. You can work with top open-source projects and get paid fast.

Owocki explained,

> One of the things that we're trying to design is giving people optionality for work that they're going to do while allowing them to test drive relationships before they decide to go full time and before they decide to get hitched. By doing a bounty with the counterparty, you're really able to try before you buy. And I think that's an important component of the ecosystem that we're building.[13]

Conclusion

The introduction of the Internet has changed the world in many ways, but perhaps its greatest impact has been in fostering collaboration across boundaries previously thought insurmountable. We can now connect not just potential collaborators on another continent but also connect with amateurs or hobbyists who are sitting on creative, unusual solutions. Blockchain promises to take this radical networking to the next level. By enhancing the power of open source, it will change the way we think about exchange, cooperation, and connection.

DADA Collective: Cromomaniaco, Chile / Lissette San Martin, Chile, collaboratively created using blockchain technology, a visual conversation.

---

[13]Ibid.

CHAPTER 6

DADA Collective: Mar Espi, Spain / Ophelia Fu, UK, collaboratively created using blockchain technology, a visual conversation.

The Value of Trust: How Much Is Peace of Mind Worth?

Do you trust me?

What do bankers, lawyers, insurers, accountants, and real estate agents have in common? (And no this isn't the start of a joke!) They are all "trusted intermediaries," or people who we pay and trust with a lot of money over the course of our lives.

Enter blockchain. When we hand over large sums of our money to trusted intermediaries, the question arises: how much can we trust them with? Can't there be a better way than handing over money to strangers?

In 2019, we are living in a crisis of trust! Pew Research Center has published more than 30 pieces of trust-related research recently, and the picture it paints is dire.[1] To put it mildly, here in the United States, we have trust issues.

Our trust in corporations and other institutions has eroded significantly.[2] We don't trust our government and we don't trust each other, which is getting in the way of our ability to solve problems.[3] We can't even agree on what's true. According to Pew, "Many Americans say the creation and spread of made-up news and information are causing significant harm to the nation and need to be stopped."[4]

The trust issues are likely here to stay. Young Americans are less trusting of other people—and key institutions—than their elders.[5]

Globally speaking, the situation is not much better. According to Pew Research Center, "Public confidence in the responsiveness, accountability, and effectiveness of elected institutions has been mired at historic lows for more than a decade."[6] According to the Center,

---

[1]Pew Research Center. 2020. "Trust, Facts and Democracy Public Attitudes about the Role of Information in Society." https://www.pewresearch.org/topics/trust-facts-and-democracy/.

[2]L. Rainie and A. Perrin. 2019. "Key Findings about Americans' Declining Trust in Government and Each Other." https://www.pewresearch.org/fact-tank/2019/07/22/key-findings-about-americans-declining-trust-in-government-and-each-other/.

[3]Ibid.

[4]G. Stocking. 2019. "Many Americans Say Made-Up News Is a Critical Problem That Needs to Be Fixed." https://www.journalism.org/2019/06/05/many-americans-say-made-up-news-is-a-critical-problem-that-needs-to-be-fixed/.

[5]J. Gramlich. 2019. "Young Americans Are Less Trusting of Other People – and Key Institutions – Than Their Elders." https://www.pewresearch.org/fact-tank/2019/08/06/young-americans-are-less-trusting-of-other-people-and-key-institutions-than-their-elders/

[6]M. Dimock. 2018. "Our Expanded Focus on Trust, Facts and the State of Democracy." https://www.pewresearch.org/2018/04/26/our-expanded-focus-on-trust-facts-

The role of evidence and facts in describing public events and shaping policy debates is persistently challenged. And as citizens become their own curators in a saturated and disaggregated information environment, the concept of a shared truth, upon which everyone can agree, appears increasingly elusive.[7]

There are many ways to improve our capacity for trust in the world and in our lives. For example, Neil Pasricha, a Canadian author, entrepreneur, podcaster, and public speaker known for his advocacy of positivity and simple pleasures, offers just three.

- One, we trust finite over infinite. It's especially true in our current era, in which we are constantly overwhelmed with infinite choices. Therefore, Apple only offers six choices for computers.
- Two, we trust humans over algorithms. Though we are increasingly surrounded by bots, we crave handshakes, smiles, and human interactions—all of which are increasingly rare.
- Three, we trust when others before us go all in and lead the way. In other words, "The more chips you push into the middle, the more we buy your hand."[8]

Blockchain offers another model to improve trust all around us: a distributed trust. It offers a trust-based system without any individuals in the system to trust or trust each other. When you combine the openness of the Internet with the security of cryptography, the result is built-in trust by design. Using examples from news and entertainment, commerce, politics, and law and government, this chapter shows how entrepreneurs are increasingly providing trust by default as a service using blockchain technology.

News and Entertainment

To say that the news and entertainment industry have trust problems is an understatement. Fake news, a neologism that refers to fabricated news with

---

and-the-state-of-democracy/.

[7]Ibid.

[8]N. Pasricha and F. Warren. 2019. "Building Trust in Distrustful Times, SXSW 2019." https://www.youtube.com/watch?v=oOIsBN_-xcY.

no basis in facts though presented as being factually accurate, is a defining phenomenon of our times. Many Americans cannot effectively distinguish between factual and opinion statements in the news.[9] In the last few years, references to and outrage around fake news have become so common that railing against fake news has become a bipartisan cultural phenomenon that has characterized our contemporary politics and culture.

Some believe that blockchain can be used to bring trust back to news and entertainment and ultimately obliterate fake news. Henry Newman, CEO and CTO of Instrumental, writes about this potential in Enterprise Storage Forum:

> What if every audio or video app on your phone, TV news camera, or your video camera automatically came set-up to create blockchains that included information such as geolocation, date and time? Editing programs would also be required to use blockchain. And what if every frame that was edited had a blockchain describing what changes were made?

Fighting Fake News

Some start-ups are taking on fake news.[10] PUBLIQ[11] is a free app for sharing digital content news and articles in which authors are rewarded according to their PUBLIQ Score, an evaluation based on reader views and feedback built on top of the DECENT network.[12] PUBLIQ uses blockchain and artificial intelligence to build a censorship-proof platform operated by authors, journalists, bloggers, and advertisers. It aims to build a rewarding process that incentivizes writing quality content. All profits made through the platform are distributed among content providers.

---

[9]M. Barthel. 2018. "Distinguishing Between Factual and Opinion Statements in the News." https://www.journalism.org/2018/06/18/distinguishing-between-factual-and-opinion-statements-in-the-news/.

[10]H. Newman. 2017. "Blockchain Could Help Stop Fake News." https://www.enterprisestorageforum.com/storage-management/blockchain-could-help-stop-fake-news.html.

[11]More information about PUBLIQ is available at https://publiq.network/ and https://decent.ch/blog/decent-network-introduces-publiq/. See also D. Ngo. 2017. "Publiq Launches Blockchain-based Content Platform for Genuine, Unbiased News." https://coinjournal.net/publiq-blockchain-content-platform/.

[12]More information about DECENT network is available at https://decent.ch/.

PUBLIQ also has a reputation-scoring system based on readers' views and feedback. Finally, in addition to battling fake news and bias reporting, PUBLIQ also offers an intermediary-free experience to advertisers (although, of course, digital advertising is another area with questionable trust issues that should be transformed).

Similarly, Civil[13] wants to use blockchain to fund quality journalism. It also helps media groups achieve financial sustainability. Again, the primary goal is to combat fake news. Civil aims to increase trust in journalism and to be a new media ecosystem that runs on a token called CVL. Using blockchain allows Civil to decentralize the power over what constitutes ethical journalism, giving token owners—readers—a voice, who can use tokens to object.

Commerce

Trust in our corporations is also low. Facebook, Amazon, Microsoft, Google, and Apple (FAMGA) are increasingly under scrutiny, and not just for their role in enabling and proliferating fake news. The tech sector is extremely valuable and most of its value is concentrated in FAMGA. The concentration of so much value has a major negative impact on innovation. Among other things, these companies have been accused of growing too big, stifling innovation, and engaging in predatory practices.[14]

You only must watch 10 minutes of Mark Zuckerberg's 2018 Congressional testimony to get a taste of the American people's distrust of

[13]More information about Civil is available at https://civil.co/.

[14]L. Kerner. 2019. "CryptoWinter Has Nothing on FAMGA Winter Market Cap Loss." https://medium.com/crypto-oracle/cryptowinter-has-nothing-on-famga-winter-market-cap-loss-501f1e4e3f1f; L. Kerner. 2018. "Why Crypto's a Growing Threat to FAMGA (a.k.a. Facebook, Apple, Microsoft, Google and Amazon)." https://medium.com/crypto-oracle/why-cryptos-a-growing-threat-to-famga-a-k-a-facebook-apple-microsoft-google-and-amazon-ea237570d3ea; L. Kerner. 2019. "The Coming Epic Battle between Crypto & FAMGA." https://www.slideshare.net/loukerner2/the-coming-epic-battle-between-crypto-famga; L. Kerner. 2018. "The Coming Epic Battle between Crypto & FAMGA (aka Facebook, Apple, Microsoft, Google, & Amazon)." https://medium.com/crypto-oracle/the-coming-epic-battle-between-crypto-famga-aka-facebook-apple-microsoft-google-amazon-1a05489c3abb; L. Kerner. 2018. "The Profound Implications of Five Increasingly Dominant Tech Companies." https://medium.com/crypto-oracle/facebook-apple-microsoft-google-amazon-aka-famga-is-eating-the-world-d3ba0c62df8b.

Zuckerberg and Facebook. There is a widespread public perception that Zuckerberg and Facebook are transactionally focused and put profit before people and relationships. Their perceived inconsistency, lack of transparency, and disrespect for users' privacy have destroyed trust in their product and possibly even in Internet businesses generally.

That is why Zuckerberg and Facebook, and their related entities such as Libra, make periodic field trips to the U.S. Congress. Our economy works because people and businesses trust each other.[15] Thus, trust is important—essential even—for your business and brand. It helps to manage relationships with customers, clients, employees, media, and numerous other marketplace stakeholders.[16]

Meet Tanjila Islam, CEO of Tiger-Trade and TradeFlo,[17] two companies that connect buyers and sellers from over 60 countries that trust their promise of high-value, curated discounted merchandise. Her entire business is about building trust, and she sees blockchain to help her build further trust.

Islam says,

I've always had a passion for international economic development. My family is originally from Bangladesh. I was born and grew up in Saudi Arabia. I'm constantly flying back and forth between many countries on the dash. I was always really shocked by the economic disparities between different countries, and I became passionate about finding ways to address them.

Islam continues,

After I finished my master's degree, I implemented programs in emerging markets, mostly across Asia. When people talk about day-to-day poverty alleviation, the normal public rhetoric, they

---

[15]S. Porat. 2017. "Why Trust Is a Critical Success Factor for Businesses Today." https://www.forbes.com/sites/theyec/2017/07/07/why-trust-is-a-critical-success-factor-for-businesses-today/#35042cdb5df0.

[16]See "Use Case: EY Hired to Help Develop Blockchain-Based Fine Wine Trading Platform." http://www.blockchaincompany.info/post/8409875/use-case-ey-hired-to-help-develop-blockchain-based-fine-wine-tra.

[17]T. Islam. Discussions with the author. 2019. More information about TigerFlo is available at https://www.tradeflo.io.

tend to focus on microfinance. But that doesn't really create broad-scale economic growth. If you look at the industrial revolution here in the United States or Europe or even in China and India, great growth comes from industries that can generate large-scale opportunities. That's what I was focused on doing. My projects had a lot of different components including the building and re-building of infrastructure, access to finance, and training.

She observes,

And, it always included an element of bringing together buyers and sellers. We put together this massive program over a few years. But we were seeing the most impact where we connected local businesses and manufacturers to international buyers and international markets.

She remembers,

The last project I did involved organizing and managing massive trade fairs in Afghanistan. They were the largest public events since the Russians invaded. They generated millions of dollars in commerce. And I was blown away because there's a demand for products from these countries and somehow it is not happening on its own. The same happens in countries like Indonesia or Vietnam.

Islam explains,

The issue is market access. So that's when I came up with the idea for my first business, Tiger-Trade. I wanted to bring international trade online. I launched it as an online marketplace connecting buyers and sellers. We're focused with our manufacturers throughout Southeast Asia on buyers in the United States and throughout Europe. I realized that we were building the marketplace.

She noticed,

The key issue is trust. Companies like Target and Walmart were specifically looking for trading partners in these emerging markets. But they wanted to find manufacturers that they could trust. We realized that we could help with that. And that's what we did.

We have relationships and know these companies. We also gave an opportunity for buyers and sellers to meet each other online.

Islam noticed,

At the same time, companies started coming to us to buy and sell their excess inventory. For example, a manufacturer would come to us with a cancellation for a brand with 60,000 men's polos that are rotting in the back. So, on the side, I launched another platform focused singularly on the international trade of excess inventory and sustainability. Did you know that a huge amount of excess inventory is burned or thrown away because it is hard to resell it?

She explains,

We provided an environmentally responsible solution to finding new markets for these products. And while the original sourcing platform involved opening market access on the excess inventory platform, we were doing full-trade transaction. We had to verify all vendors. There was a much deeper due diligence on our part to make sure transactions took place.

According to Islam, when you're doing the actual transaction, you must really understand who this is? What is their experience? Can they deliver on their obligations? Islam says,

It was a massive process and we became a trusted broker mediating each of these transactions. We had companies in Mexico and Turkey that never met but wanted to enter into a transaction quickly. We provided the element of trust to help them get there.

One of the biggest obstacles to international trade, she explains, is trust. If you are testing another company halfway around the world, you're agreeing to pay a stranger thousands of miles away to produce and ship merchandise according to your specifications. The company on the other side of the world, whether they're manufacturing or distributing, is also depending on trust, in effect agreeing to manufacture or ship a product in exchange for payment from, you, a stranger thousands of miles away. That is a lot of trust between two strangers who have never met, will never meet, and might not even speak the same language! Because of the opportunities for mistrust on both sides, a lot of transactions never even take place.

Islam continues,

To create trust, companies have to produce and verify a series of documents to represent the different stages of this process. Some are purchase order, invoice, inspection, certification, and insurance to report on payments and shipping. This document exchange process itself involves a significant investment of trust as well. There are a lot of opportunities for fraud in the process. We can help with this challenge, especially in emerging markets, at a reasonable speed and price.

She continues,

Then I looked at blockchain. This is the technology that we've really been waiting for. International trade is a series of complex, paper-intensive, multiparty transactions with a risk of fraud at every step. Obviously, the technology that we were using before was not able to support this field adequately. We still have a lot of business processes going through e-mail. Blockchain is the best solution to create efficiencies.

Islam explains,

Blockchain brings these parties together in real time and allows us to verify companies much more quickly and accurately. We are building a solution so that we can verify and certify better. For example, we can verify with the banking or government authorities the status of their business as well as that of other trading partners. Blockchain improves the otherwise cumbersome reference checking process and creates an auditable trail of all certifications and attestations.

Blockchain greatly improves trust between the buyer and seller and thus facilitates the commercial process. There's a much higher degree of transparency in the relationship with blockchain. The due diligence is expedited. The parties are now able to move forward more directly and more quickly. They can also take a closer look at the documentation and data, if they want, after certain conditions are met and approvals are granted. Using blockchain, we can create even more trust. This trusted partnership then takes these due diligence processes from 3 months down to 1 week or less. This deeper dive can be done immediately to identify trusted partners.

According to Islam, just like with energy, where it cannot flow, things break down. It's the same thing with the global economy today. We live in abundance. But the issue with the way the system has been set up until now is that it does not allow for the movement of goods and money in a way that benefits everyone. She explains, "We have been building a system to unblock it for a while. And now we are doing it with powerful technology that will take our solution to the next level."

Islam says,

We have partnered with IBM to get there. We've been working with them to help us with the business model design. They have done so many use cases and different Proof Of Concepts (POC) with blockchain. We also joined their accelerator and are working with them on integrating some of the existing technologies and projects.

Other companies are also actively working to improve trust in various verticals, such as supply chain, advertising, marketplaces, and numerous others. For example, Bext 360 provides a traceable fingerprint on commodities from producer to consumer "to liberate supply chains from opacity and inefficiency."[18] Using blockchain, Lucidity[19] inserts

---

[18]More information about Bext 360 is available at bext360.com. See also A. Knapp. 2018. "AgTech Blockchain Startup Bext360 Raises $3.35 Million to Provide Traceability to Commodities." https://www.forbes.com/sites/alexknapp/2018/06/01/agtech-blockchain-startup-bext360-raises-3-35-million-to-provide-traceability-to-commodities/#6fd484e86d25; L. Kolodny. 2017. "Bext360 Is Using Robots and the Blockchain to Pay Coffee Farmers Fairly." https://techcrunch.com/2017/04/11/bext360-is-using-robots-and-the-blockchain-to-pay-coffee-farmers-fairly/; R. Hackett. 2017. "How This Startup Plans to Use Blockchain to Revolutionize the Coffee Supply Chain." https://fortune.com/2017/10/24/blockchain-coffee-bext360/; D. Takashi. 2017. "Bext360 Aims to Transform the Global Coffee Supply Chain with Blockchain and AI." https://venturebeat.com/2017/04/11/bext360-aims-to-transform-the-global-coffee-supply-chain-with-blockchain-and-ai/.
[19]More information about Lucidity is available at lucidity.tech. See also, A. Ha. 2018. "Lucidity Uses the Blockchain to Bring More Transparency to Online Ads." https://techcrunch.com/2018/04/10/lucidity/; J. Siegel. 2018. "Lucidity Adds $5M to Deliver Its Blockchain Protocol to Digital Advertisers." https://www.builtinla.com/2018/08/15/blockchain-startup-lucidity-announces-strategic-funding.

transparency into digital advertising so that brands can be sure that they get what they pay for. TraDove[20] is a business-to-business social network that allows buyers and sellers of products and services to verify their potential partner's legitimacy and check whether they are a scam. Buyers and sellers on TraDove are reviewed and vetted to make sure that all payments and transactions are completed safely and securely. Its blockchain payment network supports international transactions, which present their own unique risks.

Politics

Whether at the root of the trust crisis, or another area in which the crisis plays out, today's politics are rife with mistrust, distrust, and a general sense that the other side is acting in bad faith. Whereas electoral politics, especially at the national level, used to be an exercise in bridging differences and working together across ideological differences, today's politics are more polarized than ever, with each side increasingly unwilling and unlikely to trust that the other is honest and has their best interest at heart.

This lack of trust is perhaps most evident in one of the most contentious arenas of national politics, and one that also shapes it, elections. Republican politicians worry that the integrity of our elections will be compromised by people voting in the United States who shouldn't be and have put in place strict "Voter ID laws." Democratic politicians accuse their Republican colleagues of seeking to suppress certain voters and accuse them of allowing foreign actors to undermine the integrity of our elections.

Voting on a Candidate

Blockchain may present a solution to overcoming this tremendous crisis in trust that has stalled creating a more efficient and effective election system in which it is easier, rather than more difficult, to vote. Nimit

---

[20]More information about TraDove is available at https://www.tradove.com/login.

Sawhney, CEO of Voatz,[21] a mobile, blockchain-based elections platform that facilitates remote voting using smartphones, says,

> Voatz is a new elections company. I use the word "new" because compared to other election companies, we are new. We're just about 4 years old. The premise of the platform is to let people vote using a smartphone with the help of biometrics, and then using blockchain in new and interesting ways to secure the process.

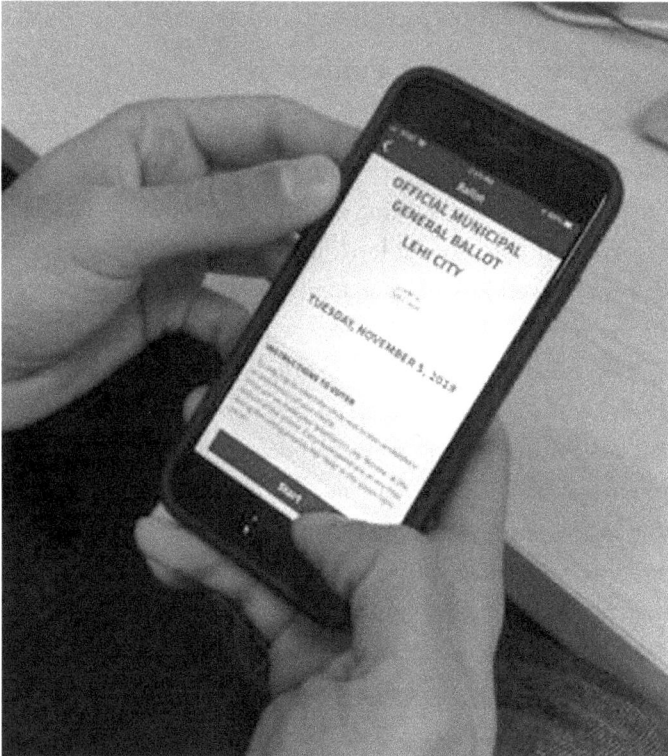

A voter begins voting on their ballot on a smartphone using the Voatz platform.

---

[21]N. Sawhney. Discussions with the author. 2019. More information about Voatz is available at https://voatz.com/. See also, C. Loizos. 2019. "Voatz, the Blockchain-based Voting App, Gets Another Vote of Confidence as Denver Agrees to Try It." https://techcrunch.com/2019/03/07/voatz-the-blockchain-based-voting-app-gets-another-vote-of-confidence-as-denver-agrees-to-try-it/; M. Kelly. 2018. "Nearly 150 West Virginians Voted with a Mobile Blockchain App." https://www.theverge.com/2018/11/10/18080518/blockchain-voting-mobile-app-west-virginia-voatz.

According to Sawhney, the process for the voters usually begins much like the normal absentee voting process. You fill out an absentee request form, send it to your county or city clerk, they approve it, and then provision you as a voter. Then, you get a notification to download the app on your iPhone or Android phone and can go through the verification process, in which you take a picture of an ID alongside your face. It uses facial recognition, and once your face is matched to your ID, you can access your ballot on the phone and submit your ballot. It gets anonymized and then submitted to the network, where it lands on the blockchain network and remains locked until election day when the clerks unlock it and count your vote.

Sawhney recalls,

We formally got started in 2015 after we won a hackathon at South by Southwest in Austin in 2014. The premise was to create a new elections platform from the ground up, one which focuses on security and accessibility using mobile devices, biometrics, and then uniquely uses blockchain to provide additional levels of security and is tamper-resistant. We've done about 53 elections so far, our most high-profile of which was last year.

He continues,

We did two elections in West Virginia. One was in the primary for two counties, which was then extended to 24 counties for the general election. In March 2019, we were selected by the city and county of Denver to offer remote voting to overseas and military citizens. We are doing that election right now as we speak. Additionally, Utah County (Utah), Jackson County (Oregon), and Umatilla County (Oregon) are the latest jurisdictions to select Voatz for their 2019 elections. Utah County is also the first jurisdiction in the United States to expand this mobile voting initiative to citizens with disabilities so that they too can vote in an accessible manner without needing to give up their privacy.

According to Sawhney, "Voting is the loudest voice a citizen has. But with long lines and outdated systems, it can be a frustrating and time-consuming exercise." Voatz creates the convenience of voting anywhere in 60 seconds or less. "Using biometric identification with total privacy and anonymity, you can have the confidence that your vote is accurately recorded. You'll never need to stand in a polling line again using Voatz. You can vote in public elections, ballot initiatives, budget decisions, college elections, corporate governance, shareholder meetings, or anywhere else. Voatz offers secure, tamper-free voting via a smartphone, multisource ID verification, advanced biometrics, and blockchain-based reputability.

From the time the voter submits the ballot, the voter remains anonymous and the ballot is stored on blockchain until it's time to tabulate. Every single mobile ballot produces a formatted, printable paper ballot. When it's time to tabulate, officials from the jurisdiction unlock the digital lockbox, print all the mobile votes on the ballot paper, and then scan and tabulate them alongside the rest of the jurisdiction's ballots."

iPhone Screenshots

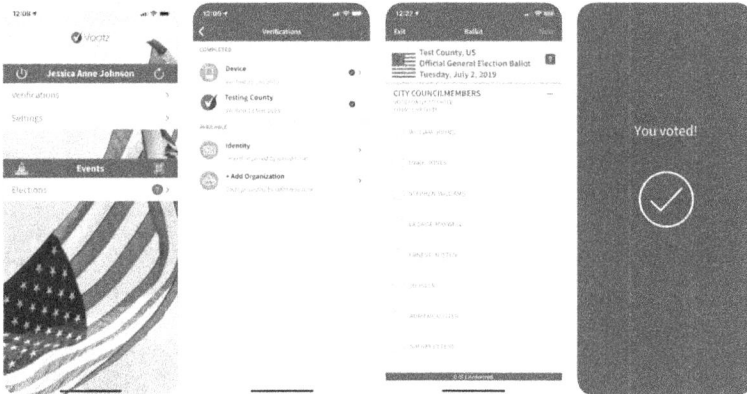

The Voatz homescreen; the Voatz verifications screen; a sample ballot, ready for voting on the Voatz platform; and a success screen after securely, successfully submitting a vote using Voatz.

He explains,

One of the unique features of Voatz is that every voter, once they vote, receives a voter-verifiable digital receipt. It's anonymized and password-protected, and an anonymized copy is also sent to the jurisdiction. This way, the voter can verify their selections, and after the election, the jurisdiction can confirm that what's on the receipt matches the printed, tabulated official ballot, alongside the data stored on blockchain. This allows the jurisdiction to confirm that the system tabulated the votes properly and that all tabulated ballots matched voter intent. It's a great way to rollout trust and demonstrates to people how this can be a better, more trusted way to vote than they do right now. Voting over e-mail, fax, or mail, which are the current options offered to overseas citizens, presents problems. This demographic is our primary focus as we expand our absentee voting program.

Regarding Voatz's use of blockchain, Sawhney explains,

We use blockchain primarily as a data security and auditing tool. Essentially, it's used to store the ballot data, and the benefit is that it doesn't have a single point of failure. It's hard to destroy the system in that if a single node survives, the election will continue.

The type of blockchain we are using is Hyperledger Fabric, a public-permissioned network. This is useful to us because we wanted to mirror how elections are conducted in the physical world, where we can ensure that all nodes are properly secured and ratified. They must be within the jurisdictional boundaries of the United States, meaning no foreign actor can be a system administrator. Every entity touching it, including staff and our staff, must go through access checks. We then also have a set of external auditors, including one of the three-letter agencies, perform a full audit before the general election. Then again after the general election to make sure everything went well. This hybrid architecture is useful, where, even though it's not public, anybody can see what's happening.

According to Sawhney, with such new technology especially surrounding an election, you don't want to offer something that most people don't understand.

More than 98 percent of people still don't understand how blockchain works. There's a lot of misinformation, so we are focusing more on mobile voting, which uses blockchain in a unique and simple way. We're not letting people vote on a web browser. You must use a native mobile application, or, in some cases, you can use a tablet as well.

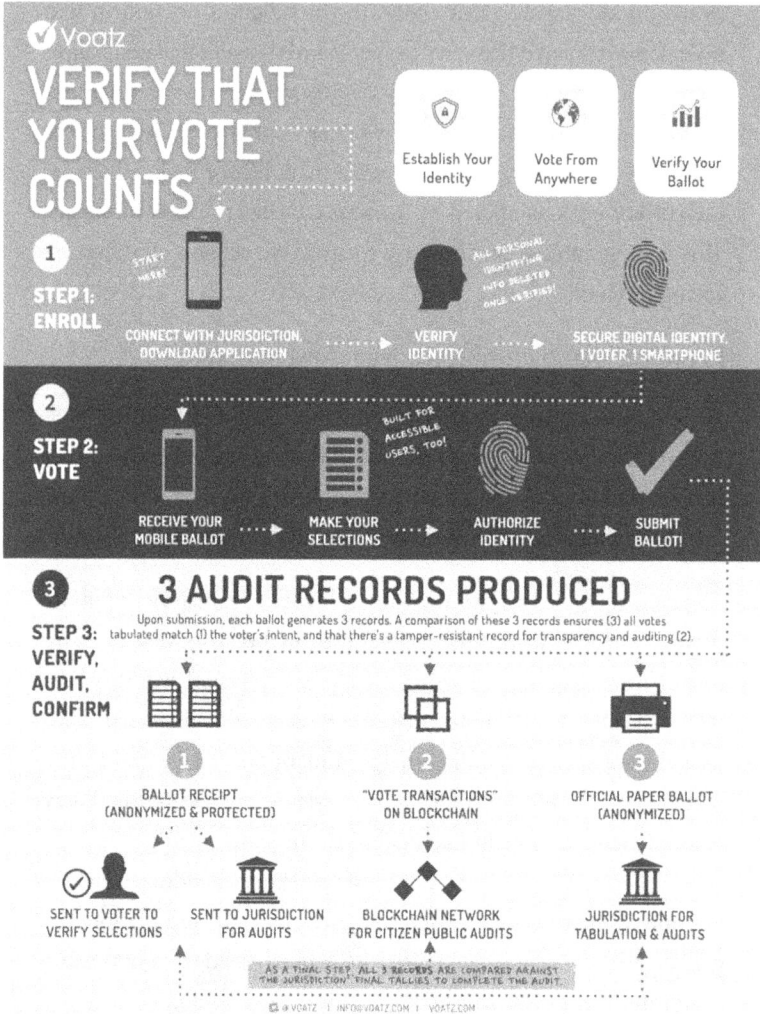

Voatz system works end-to-end: from verification, to voting, to the post-election audit. Follow the dotted lines to understand how a voter gets verified, submits their ballot, and how jurisdictions tabulate, and audit all submitted ballots.

If you want to roll out something like this, which concerns something as sensitive as our elections, it needs to be done in a slow, gradual manner taking baby steps. We need to make sure we build trust along the way, educate in a proper manner, and refine our product as we go.

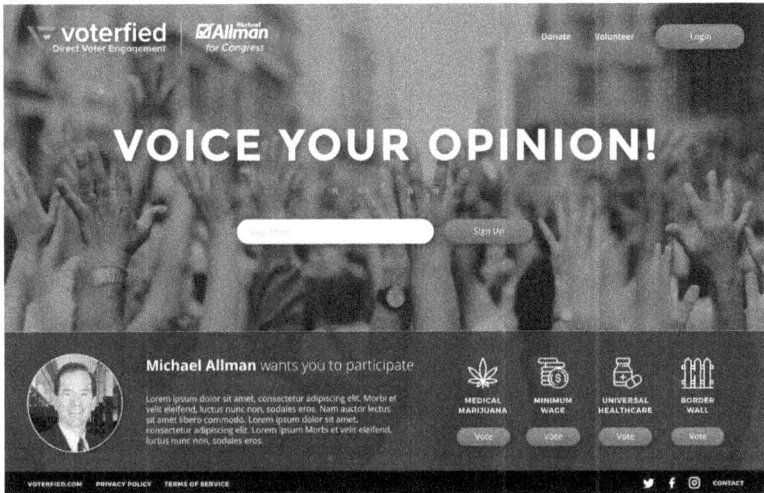

Sample home page powered by Voterfied, Version 2.0.

Sawhney explains, "We don't want it to become too big before people actually understand some of the basics of how it's working."

He says,

> The promise of mobile technology is often overlooked. The phone, especially iPhones and the newer Android devices, are in many ways a lot safer than your average computer or desktop or a laptop. And similarly, voting on a native app is quite safe.

Voting on an Issue

Not all voting is done to choose a single candidate. Sometimes the question at hand is a specific issue, not a candidate.

Very simply, Voterfied[22] is an online software platform that helps elected officials and candidates interact with their voters. It does so by offering an online voting system where constituents vote on issues. A candidate for office or an elected official has a dedicated website where they can post information and questions and seek input from their constituents. The platform verifies that users are registered to vote in the appropriate election district. A voter can go online, sign up once, and easily express their opinion. Blockchain comes in to record that vote and make sure it's immutable.

---

[22]More information about Voterfied is available at https://www.voterfied.com.

The voters know instantaneously that their voice was heard. They can see when they voted on an issue. They can see the current count. With all the benefits of electronic voting, they can change their mind. It can be anonymous. The platform can make it seamless to express their opinion.

Allman explains,

We find that voters are frustrated today. They want to be engaged but don't know how. Nobody wants to go to town halls that often end up in shouting matches. Send your congressman an e-mail and you get nothing useful back. You try to call, but you can't get through.

He continues,

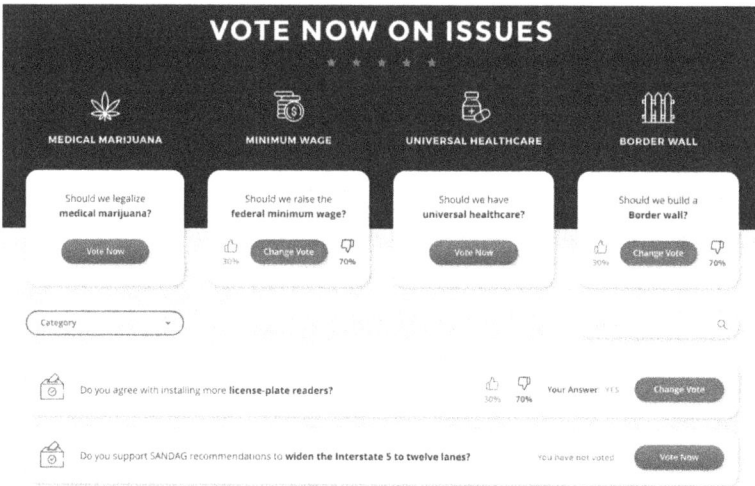

Sample page of demo Voterfied site with questions and what it would look like to show a user's vote.

Now, for the first time, they can express their opinion and have it heard. And most importantly, the elected official or candidate now knows where their voters stand. It is an opportunity to replace polling. It is effectively a much less expensive and more immediate method of polling. It facilitates direct engagement with voters. It means that as a politician you can differentiate yourself. You can listen to your voters, and Voterfied will help you get elected.

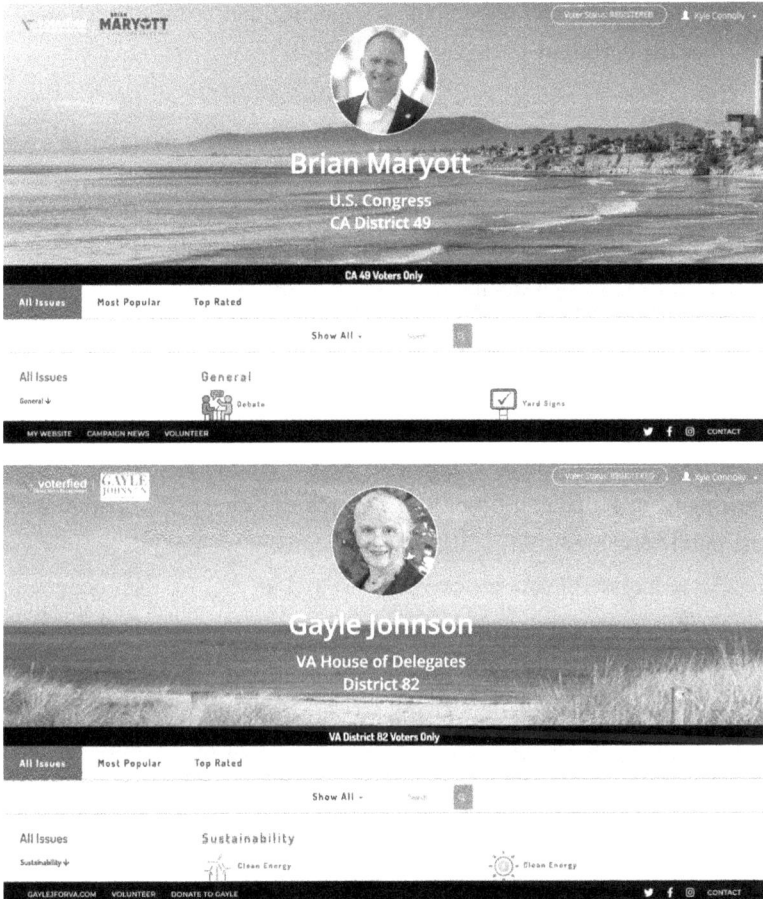

Gayle Johnson for Virginia Delegate Home Page and Brian Maryott for Congress, California Home Page.

According to Allman,

That's how we're using blockchain. Voterfied is a way to allow for confidential voting and facilitate an open distributed database that can be audited and can build trust. We are built on Hyperledger. There's no coin or cryptocurrency. We're finding two big benefits to that. Number one, it's branded for the politician, who are our customers. They drive voters to their Voterfied site, and voters interact by voting and commenting. We've worked on focus groups. Voters get a good feeling after they interact with the tool. Also, the candidate gets access to important data to help them run a better campaign. We also see the application in other contexts such as running corporate or organization boards.

He says,

Our democracy platform lets you voice your opinions to candidates and elected officials through blockchain voting. Just sign up, get validated, and you can demand more from your politicians. First, you'll need to sign up and get verified to create an account with a name, associated e-mail, and password. You will then receive an e-mail from your politician with a link to verify your e-mail address. After that, we confirm that you are a registered voter.

"This verification ensures that your elected officials know that they are hearing from actual constituents. We match the voter's information with the public voter registration list in your county."

According to Allman, once a voter is logged in, they see their politician's name, jurisdiction, and picture. They can scroll down and look through all the issues in their community. Once a voter selects a question that they want to voice their opinion on, they will see that each topic provides arguments for and against, along with links to articles to help them make the most informed decision. When the voter is ready to decide, they click on the screen and vote.

Article from the San Diego Union Tribune.

Voters get instant confirmation that their vote has been counted. If they change their mind, they also have the freedom to change their vote at any time. The goal is to modernize democracy and empower citizens to participate. This can lead to more government transparency and the ability to hold politicians accountable.

Our trust issues run rampant in our politics, and one reason for it is a lack of communication. The public feels alienated and like their representatives don't understand how they feel—because often they don't. The public isn't wrong in feeling that their voices aren't heard. Blockchain can make it possible to connect constituents to their representatives—elected or seeking election—and ensure that the public's voices are heard. In other words, it can slowly begin the process of restoring trust back into our politics.

Laws and Government

The trust problem with government isn't limited to the relationship between the public and the elected officials. Within government, there is a real crisis of confidence as well. Our entire legal and political structures are in some ways built on a foundation of trust, and the growing gulf of trust between government officials, lawyers, and their partners threaten the most basic aspect of our society.

Real Estate, Better

Chao Cheng-Shorland is CEO and co-founder of ShelterZoom,[23] a real-time, multiparty platform that allows for secure online contract negotiations. Their technology and analytics also make it possible for contracts to be ported across transactions and data-mined for greater control over the different components of a contract. They refer to this as the "Contract of Things (CoT)." Just as the Internet of Things (IoT) is a way for devices to "talk" to one another, CoT is a blockchain-based way to analyze contracts across many different transactions and make contracts interactive rather than siloed documents.

---

[23]C. Cheng-Shorland. Discussions with the author. 2019. More information about ShelterZoom is available at https://www.shelterzoom.com.

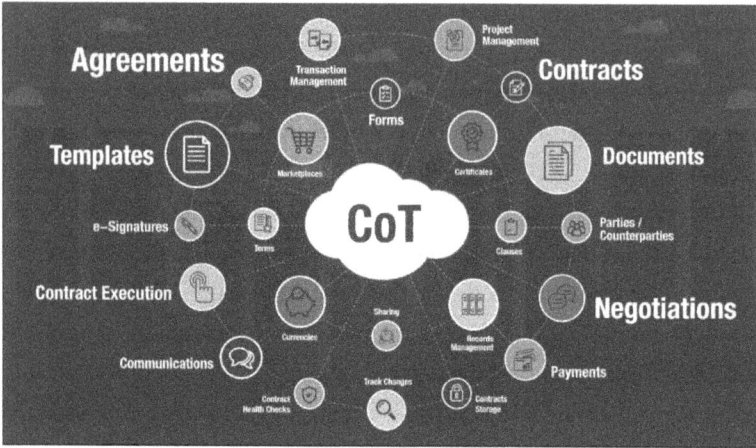

The many components of a contract can now be analyzed and ported across transactions using ShelterZoom blockchain-based technology.

One of the company's first products was OfferNow—a way to harness blockchain technology to make the property sales process more transparent and secure. She says,

> I met my business partner almost 3 years ago. He is a real estate broker and very deep on the business side. His whole family has been involved in real estate for a century. He's very forward-thinking and creative on the business side. He always has a vision. What he was lacking before was knowledge of the technology. He never met anyone from the technology field. I met him through a mutual friend.

She continues,

> I knew he was looking for someone, and I knew I was too. I thought about real estate before I even met him. I was thinking about how the industry wants to change. It was really antiquated with so much manual processing.

Cheng-Shorland reflects, "We are not a blockchain business. We are a blockchain-enabled business." According to Cheng-Shorland,

> At the end of the day, scalability, profitability, and how you get traction are all important. It all comes down to the business model. And relatedly, the roadmap. We are very clear on what

companies should be delivering at each stage to be positioned for future growth. We strategize at every step.

She explains,

We scanned the market, and that's how we found the offer and acceptance. And there is really a gap in the market. We looked at the U.S. market and at Australia, China, Japan, and England. We concluded that the one common thing missing is a consumer-facing offer and acceptance process and platform. That's how we nailed our initial scope. If we have an offer and acceptance platform and are going to make people use our system, we decided not to create a shelterzoom.com and ask everyone to come to our website. It would take time to build both technically and reputationally with SEO credibility.

Cheng-Shorland says,

We decided to provide a little button, and everyone can just quickly plug it in as a widget on their website. All our branding says that it is powered by blockchain. We thought that this would lead to quicker adoption. We thought it would be wonderful to enable anyone to buy or rent a house by pressing a button. That's our business model. It's around pressing a button to buy or rent property online. Regardless of where you are in the world, what nationality you are, what race you are, everyone should be able to do that.

According to Cheng-Shorland,

People submit offers through the widget, upload documents, manage, offer, accept, and e-sign orders—the whole dashboard of the virtual negotiation room is powered by blockchain. The reason I say "powered by blockchain" is because we provide a widget which comes with the blockchain technology. You come to the real estate website and, if you love a house, you can make an offer just by clicking a button.

Once enabled, some information will be pre-populated because there's an integration between the site and the widget. Then you can very quickly fill in some details about you and your agent. You can go through the terms, price, loan amount, your anticipated closing date, and other information. Then you can even upload a supporting document, such as your loan prequalification. By the end, you accept the terms and conditions and submit. It's a very consumer-facing or agent-facing offer process.

Cheng-Shorland explains,

> We create a virtual negotiation room for people. You get access to a dashboard and can see where you are in the process and what has been already signed, rejected, and is under negotiation. You can see which property has multiple offers. Then you can also drill down to see the whole document flow and see what happened with each offer.

This is really where the value of blockchain comes in. Each number is one block. It creates total transparency. The buyer, the seller, the agent, everyone has an identical view and has full information about what is happening. You can pretty much see all the details and can negotiate the offer or counter offer. You can revise, reject, or sign. It's very much a manual process, but it's completely digitized. Then each step is stored on blockchain for the security, transparency, and convenience of everyone involved. Following the principles behind the CoT, it is all auditable.

Cheng-Shorland explains,

> There's just a ton of paperwork in every stage of real estate. We didn't have a real estate deal platform on the market, so we wanted to build our own. That is how we ended up giving the widget to everyone who got a property listing. We also realized that real estate is one of the most complex transaction management areas. It has many forms, multiple parties, and numerous stages. You must do a lot of steps that involve many service providers. If we can digitize real estate, then we should be able to provide this virtual negotiation room process to other industries with no problems.

Time to Upgrade You DMV Experience

According to Cheng-Shorland,

> We are starting to utilize the same technology and apply it to other industries. What we are now creating is the entire deal contract

and transaction management platform on blockchain. This is our second platform. The real estate platform was our first. Everything is digital. Paper is no longer needed at any stage of the contract negotiation. It's all in the system. Now they use DocuSign for signature but the form itself is very much paper-based. It's just scanned or OCR'd. It's not really a true negotiation of a contract or a digitally managed transaction.

Bernie Moreno is the founder and chairman of Ownum,[24] a block-chain tech company focused on unlocking business growth and making government more efficient by focusing on car titles at this time. He says,

The digital economy has created great things. But it has also created a lot of problems. What most governments do is put their data in a bubble. And the challenge it presents is that the data the government holds is very valuable. They control it so tightly that it basically doesn't allow data sharing at all. So along comes blockchain to break that trust gap.
He explains,

If you go into a government agency and talk to them about block-chain, they'll say to you, after a quick Google search, "you're trying to sell me Bitcoin." I can't tell you how many times in Cleveland I hear people assume that I'm out creating my own cryptocurrency. It's a huge issue. One of the things that we've tried to do is explain new technology using old technology ideas. We have come up with this idea. We call it the "BELTED solution." So rather than saying that we are going to use blockchain to solve a problem, we talk about digitizing car titles.

---

[24]B. Moreno. Discussions with the author. 2019. More information about Ownum is available at https://www.ownum.io. See also, S. Allard. 2019. "Bernie Moreno Launches CHAMPtitle in Bid to Disrupt Auto Titling." https://www.clevescene .com/scene-and-heard/archives/2019/03/22/bernie-moreno-launches-champtitle-in-bid-to-disrupt-auto-titling; A. Westrope. 2019. "Startup Ownum's First Product Is Blockchain Vehicle Titles." https://www.govtech.com/biz/Startup-Ownums-First-Product-is-Blockchain-Vehicle-Titles.html; S. Hannan. 2018. "Chain Reaction." https://clevelandmagazine.com/in-the-cle/the-read/articles/chain-reaction.

Moreno says,

"BELTED" is an acronym for a Blockchain Encrypted Ledger That's Executable and Distributed. You get away from the idea of blockchain and its association with cryptocurrency. This looks like a marketing ploy to reframe a private blockchain or a private distributed ledger. That's the whole point! The conversation has gotten very difficult, especially when you're dealing with government authorities. It's the way blockchain has been used.

According to Moreno, "part of the hype problem is that you have a lot of vendors talking about blockchain solving everything. That creates a problem because it sews doubt. Is it just snake oil? Blockchain isn't going to solve every single problem. To get away from all this baggage, we use BELTED solution in our discussions, especially with governments, because it is a reminder that we are not talking about crypto."

Think about the idea that it is 2020 and the government still issues you a physical piece of paper that represents the fact that you own an asset. It seems like an odd concept. Let's walk through implications. Moreno explains,

My Mercedes dealership in Cleveland probably sells about 300 cars a month. We have five people that help with titling. That's all they do all day. They take this piece of paper that starts as a manufacturer's statement of origin, the paperwork that the client signs, you know where you're going into an office. You have signed a bunch of papers, take all those documents, and drive it over to a physical office and then it gets printed out as a new Ohio title.

There's more! Moreno continues,

Then it comes back. Either it gets mailed to a bank, to a leasing company, or to you, the purchaser. It's an enormous amount of work! And look at it from the lender's perspective: if you buy a car from me and finance it through the bank, I mail the bank your title and they have to receive it and process it.

He continues,

Then, if you pay off the loan, the bank must figure out that you paid for it. Take this title out of an envelope and mail it to you. In the meantime, that can take 2 or 3 weeks and a bank on average gets four or five phone calls from every client about their title. It's crazy and costs them a lot of money.

But wait, there is more, much, much more! Moreno explains,

If you've ever had a car stolen or totaled, you'll know that it takes insurance companies about 90 days to clear a claim. Most of that is because they're waiting for the ownership documents of the vehicle and it's extremely costly and cumbersome to both, the insurance companies and the car companies.

Have you received a recall notice for cars that you haven't owned since you were a kid? Yet the government puts a lot of pressure on these car companies to get these recalls done. Imagine if the car company could send a notification to your phone! "Your car has been recalled. Press here to see what it's for. Press here to make an appointment. And it's all done."

Moreno explains,

You can do that because your title now lives on a BELTED system instead of in your file folder or in a bank vault somewhere. So those are the kinds of things that we can accomplish by digitizing what used to be a physical piece of paper.

Moreno says,

I have a conundrum if I want to sell you my car. You want to buy a red car. We're good there, right? We've got video technology, we can see the condition, etc. But now I say to you, "okay, I'm going to mail you the check when you send me the title." And you say, "no, no, no, no, no. You send me the title. I'll send you the check." Then you have this conversation back and forth for a long time.

He continues,

Imagine you can send a title the same way you send a text message and through our BELTED system. It validates the sale price for the state authority and the registration fee, and the title fees clears. The sales tax transfers using the smart contract. That title goes to you and the money is transferred to the seller, all in a snap of a finger. You could also take out a loan as easily.

People define blockchain in different ways depending on their perspective. Moreno says,

> We define permissioned blockchain as a distributed system where the permissioning authority can give access to different participants in the system. The way we utilize blockchain is by distributing trust throughout the network. The most important and overlooked aspect of blockchain and smart contracts is the idea that you have a digital checklist.

He explains, "We use Hyperledger Fabric. We found it to be really the best platform. It gives us the functionality we need."

Digitizing documents allows for savings and process improvement. Moreno observes,

> In the case of our company, a car dealership, with our titles, there is a process. Consumers must validate their data, the bank validates certain data, the insurance, and more. There's an agreement among these disparate parties. With blockchain, we can have a network that automates and digitizes car titles after certain conditions are met in a way that doesn't require blind trust.

He explains,

> Think back, a long time ago, if you were traveling to Miami, I'd call a travel agency and they'd book me on a flight and send me a boarding card a couple of days before my flight. If I lost the card, I would have to figure out what to do. Somebody said, "Well, this is expensive and it's hard to purchase tickets this way, so why don't we allow people to print their boarding passes at home?" And then that kind of became the thing. And now, of course, everybody keeps their boarding pass on their phone. And with your pass on your phone, you can receive gate updates in real time. If the departure time changes, they can ping you. If the flights going to be on time, they can, again, ping you.

> For example, General Motors is a giant company. They don't know much about their car sales. They trust that their dealerships report on time and accurately. But the manufacturer is one of the

inputs, right? Unless you're in the car business, you can't appreciate how much car titles impact the ecosystem and how costly and inefficient they are.

Moreno explains,

> It's kind of like if I was opening an airline and said, "you can only travel on my planes if I mail you a card boarding pass first." I know because I've been in the car business my entire life, but car titles produce an enormous amount of friction in that ecosystem. And by friction, I mean expenses. It costs the parties in the system an enormous amount of money. So that's where we started. We can put in this system anything that's titled. We can do motorcycles, boats, RVs, things like that.

Addressing the Flavors of Fraud

Among the greatest risks of digitizing the titling process is around the possibility of fraud. Perhaps the reason progress has been slow and government bureaucrats have been so resistant to technology is that with increased efficiency slips in new opportunities for hackers to take what's not theirs. Whether through plain fraud or more creative counterfeit, blockchain addresses the security risks inherent to digitizing assets.

Guy Scott, CEO of VeriDoc Global,[25] provides blockchain-powered, QR code-based antifraud solutions to organizations to ensure they are protected against counterfeiters. He says, "I got into the IT industry back in 2007. We started building websites and then moved to student management systems in Australia. RTOs needed student management systems mostly for compliance and reporting to the government."

Scott noticed,

> ASQA made an announcement in 2015 and wanted to sePDF documents properly and verify credentials. That's how VeriDoc Global was formed. We give a document a unique hash value and add the same unique hash value on a public blockchain, which is obviously

---

[25]G. Scott. Discussions with the author. 2019. More information about VeriDoc Global is available at https://www.veridocglobal.com/.

a distributed ledger and cannot be tampered with. It is completely decentralized. And that's what brings value to our product. Because the unique hash value is on blockchain, you know that it can't be changed.

He explains,

When a QR code is scanned, it reads the link that we've embedded into the QR code. We make our own unique QR codes. We don't pull from a library of QR codes. The link that is embedded into the QR code checks the unique hash value on the document, blockchain, and client database. The QR code allows the client to ensure that it's secure.

He continues, "We then built the whole thing on Ethereum while continuing to add support for other blockchains and now we are a multi-platform solution. We work on any blockchain."

VeriDoc Global has developed an antifraud document verification system that ensures the user is looking at a true and correct document. You might have seen QR codes before. They are starting to pop up everywhere on cereal boxes and in newspapers. A QR code is a two-dimensional barcode that stores a lot more information than a regular barcode.

Scott explains,

We've embedded a QR code on a document, like an education certificate, with a hash inside this QR code. The hash holds a string of information that is then placed on the blockchain network for security verification, and, most importantly, end-user validation. The way it works is that the issuer produces an education certificate and then the system gives the education certificate a unique hash value. It then embeds that hash value as a QR code on that education certificate using a QR code reading app. All you need to do is scan the QR code of the education certificate with any smartphone and you can verify it right then and there. The app will then show you if the document you are looking at is an original or a fake.

The system looks at that hash value inside of the QR code and then checks the hash value on blockchain and displays a certificate that is linked to the hash value. The technology might sound complicated but the user experience is very simple. This stops the creation and proliferation of fake education certificates because blockchain technology prevents the data and the QR code from ever being changed or removed.

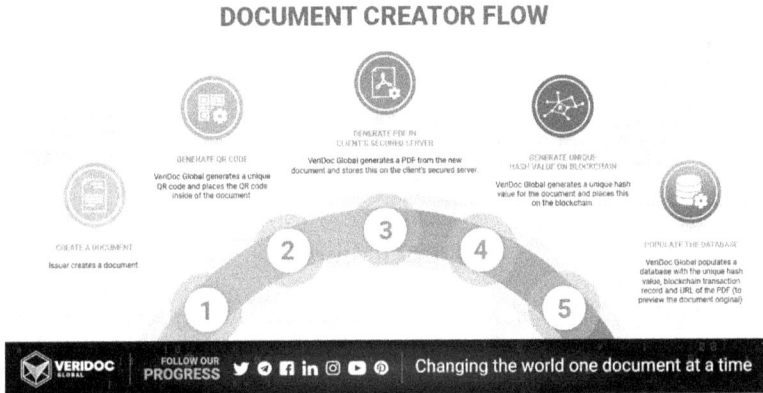

Veridoc document creator flow.

This also means that if an education certificate is ever lost or stolen, ownership of the property can still be verified on blockchain. The applications for this are endless and include passports, driver's licenses, academic certificates, bank statements, mortgage deeds, stock certificates, medical records, and legal documents. The list just continues to grow. This is the future of document security.

Scott also explains,

We developed an antifraud document verification system that ensures that the user is looking at a true and correct document created by the issuer. Most documents are printed on plain paper to try and prevent document fraud. The most common practice being used is watermarks. But it's never been easier to scan the original document and use photoshop to print out documents that look every bit as good as the original. And how can anyone tell what it is supposed to look like?

It's a problem VeriDoc Global can solve.

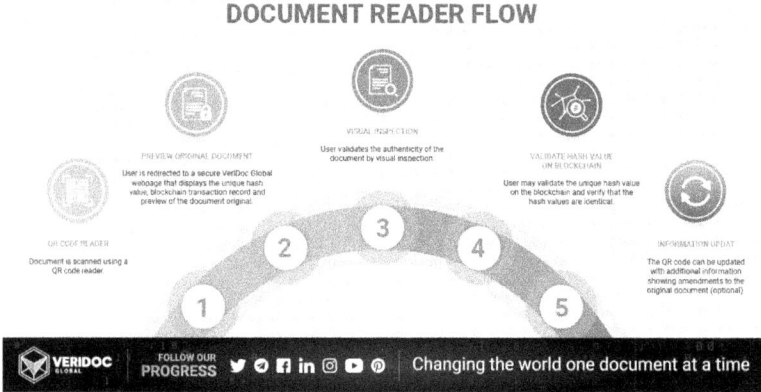

Veridoc document creator flow.

Conclusion

There has never been more communication with more people and more readily available. However, at the same time, we trust each of our information less, we trust authority less, and we trust each other less. The beauty of blockchain lies in its replacement of the need for trust.

Blockchain allows for preverification, which—by serving as a prevetted authority—lowers the barrier for trust. It's not that blockchain makes us trust one another and get along, rather it eliminates the need for trust altogether. Instead of trusting each other, we need only trust the highly secure, decentralized technology. And with ever-increasing complexity in increasingly sensitive and valuable transactions, eliminating risk is essential.

By securing our communications and interactions, blockchain replaces trust as a tie that binds. And when trust isn't an obstacle, there are boundless opportunities for making operational improvements, such as remote management and oversight of your business.

DADA Collective: Ophelia Fu, UK / Isa Kost, Italy, collaboratively created using blockchain technology, a visual conversation.

CHAPTER 7

Blockchain's Butterfly Effect: How Small, Efficient Payments Can Add Up and Make a Big Difference

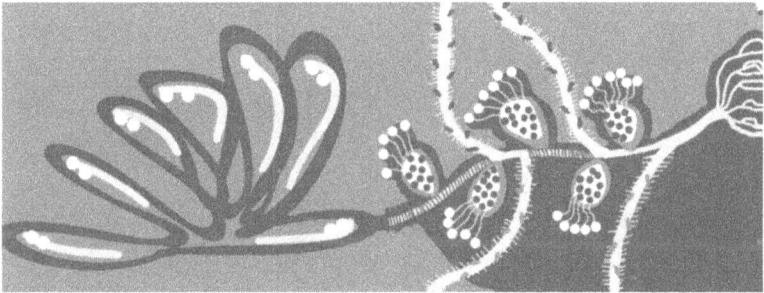

DADA Collective: Allan Ramirez, Costa Rica / Isa Kost, Italy, collaboratively created using blockchain technology, a visual conversation.

Small Things in Life

A random act of kindness, something selfless to help a stranger or just make someone's day that much better. Various communities, online and offline, encourage small acts of kindness, either spontaneous or planned.

If you google "small acts of kindness," you will find many suggestions. Too many to count, and way too many to do. Some lists and a ton of stories. Why? The answer is simple: small acts can have a big impact. I am certain you have experienced the big power of small acts of kindness in your life many times, whether you remember them or not.

The power of small is not limited to the small acts of kindness. Pause for a second and think of small changes that have made a big difference in your life. How many times have you been told about the life-changing effects of 3 to 5 minutes of meditation every day? Or how 15 minutes of walking per day can add years onto your life? Our personal lives are full of small changes that lead to a big difference.

Scientists have all sorts of names for it. Physics hails the power of the "butterfly effect" to highlight the power of small, initial actions—say a butterfly flapping its wings—on a much bigger outcome far away—like a tornado across the world. Social scientists regard the importance of a "nudge"—small interventions that have no meaningful limitations on our liberty—to produce a more favorable outcome.

The power of small, initial actions.

In the context of blockchain, tokens—a privately issued digital asset secured using cryptography with characteristics of money, such as fungible, divisible, portable, durable, and limited supply—are a flexible, powerful mechanism that can drive engagement to unleash the proverbial "butterfly effect." By aligning actions and rewards, it has the potential of becoming a powerful tool of capturing attention and shaping behavior at scale, one microaction at a time.

This alignment between actions and rewards, rooted in behavioral psychology, will have an unprecedented impact because tokens provide highly relevant and highly targeted rewards immediately. By effectively gamifying microactions, we can build powerful loyalty programs at scale for more aligned communities where individuals and participants are nudged to do the right thing—produce high-quality goods, take socially responsible actions, facilitate equality, and so on.

Of course, who will shape and capture attention and behavior at scale is critical. While time will tell, a multiway street among companies, organizations, communities, individuals, institutions, and other stakeholders is likely to unfold in the next decade or two.

Suffice it to say that life is not a social experiment. Approaching your business or life in this manner always backfires. A focus on building transparent communities and ecosystems is more likely to be sustainable.

Whatever you call it—"butterfly effect" or something else—the power of small has major implications and big value for the use of blockchain in business. As we'll see, the accumulation of small financial transactions is a powerful force.

Small Transactions Mean Business

In business, micropayments are financial transactions involving small sums of money, often less than a dollar and in some cases a fraction of a cent, that are almost always made online. For example, website purchases for ringtones, pay-per-views, downloads, e-books, and subscriptions in the $1 to $5 range would be considered micropayments.

Some micropayments are extremely small—even just cents! For example, a $0.01 payment for a download or a $0.025 payment for an SMS is an excellent example of lesser value micropayments. While the upper limit is usually $1, each company sets its own micropayment threshold. For example, PayPal considers any transaction below $10 a micropayment.

Many businesses incorporate micropayments into their business model to increase the interest of the potential global audiences and eventually attract more and more customers. For example, micropayments have been used to pay intellectual property owners when their content is downloaded. For a relatively small sum, you can download a song, picture, or other content on the Internet at any time.[1]

Blockchain Is Perfect for Payments and Financial Applications

Pennies and fractions of pennies across many people add up to a substantial amount.

At a high level, blockchain is just a giant table that keeps a track of transactions in chronological order. In the process, it facilitates trust and reduces costs. For example, BitPesa, a blockchain-based company focused on facilitating business-to-business payments in Kenya, Nigeria, and Uganda has reduced its commission amounts from 9 percent to 3 percent with blockchain.[2]

It is not a coincidence that Bitcoin is the blockchain's first application. Since Bitcoin was created in 2009, many theorized about the future of the

---

[1]L. Faulk. 2018. "The History of Micropayments." https://medium.com/@llofa/the-history-of-micropayments-e49adc495a85.

[2]A. Sergeenkov. 2018. "How Blockchain Is Changing Money Transfers." https://hackernoon.com/how-blockchain-is-changing-money-transfers-e9cb85e94932.

financial industry. Bitcoin is entirely digital; unlike fiat currencies such as USD, CAD, AUD, euros, or Japanese yen, it cannot be touched. It is also much easier to send across borders, especially in large amounts. For these reasons, anything related to money, value, and currency is likely a natural application of blockchain technology. That is why you see so many financial and bank-related applications on blockchain.[3]

Blockchain will impact many banking models that are built on facilitating payments and generally utilize banking. On the payments side, by eliminating intermediaries, blockchain can speed up payments made at lower rates than those charged by banks. With clearing and settlement, blockchain can reduce, in almost real time, transactions between financial institutions. For fundraising, blockchain can provide companies with immediate access to capital through the initial placement of coins (ICO). We saw the power of this mechanism in 2017 and 2018.

It's not just Bitcoin there are other blockchain applications in payments and banking as well. For securities, through the "tokenization" of securities, such as stocks, bonds, and alternative assets, blockchain strengthens the structure of the capital market. All transaction records are secured by cryptography and tied to previous transactions and distributed among participants in a ledger. For loans, blockchain can make borrowing money safer and provide lower interest rates by eliminating the need for credit intermediaries.[4] There are numerous other financial blockchain applications. For example, Maker provides decentralized stablecoin, collateral loans, and community governance.[5]

Other financial applications of blockchain are still emerging. For example, blockchain is making inroads in international remittance, providing people around the world rare access to fast, cheap, and unrestricted payments. Several major banks have partnered with Ripple,[6] a real-time gross settlement system, currency exchange, and remittance network blockchain-powered protocol. Ripple is built on a distributed open-source protocol and

---

[3] J. Pritchard and K. Khartit. 2020. "How Blockchain Is Changing Banking and Financial Services." https://www.thebalance.com/how-blockchain-is-changing-banking-and-financial-services-4174354.

[4] Sergeenkov. "How Blockchain Is Changing Money Transfers."

[5] More information about Maker is available at https://makerdao.com/.

[6] More information about Ripple is available at https://www.ripple.com/.

supports tokens representing fiat currency, cryptocurrency, commodities, and other units of value, such as frequent flyer miles or mobile minutes to facilitate cross-border payments. Among others, MoneyGram and Western Union have announced partnerships with Ripple. By lowering the costs of blockchain-based cryptocurrency transfers, users of blockchain can eliminate the need for banks, and in doing so, can speed up transactions and eliminate the need for banks and reduce transfer costs.[7]

Others are also taking advantage of blockchain's features to tap into the international remittances market. Stellar, an open-source and decentralized protocol for digital currency-to-fiat money transfers, allows for cross-border transactions. According to its website, it is available for "fractions of a penny."[8] Maybe Stellar will impress you with its commitment to the power of small—if you found other examples of small acts of kindness mundane! Jed McCaleb, the founder of Mt. Gox and co-founder of Ripple, launched the protocol with Joyce Kim. It is supported by The Stellar Development Foundation, a 501(c)3 nonprofit.[9] In December 2017, Stellar announced a partnership with SureRemit, a Nigeria-based noncash remittances platform, among others.[10]

Big Impact on Small Payments

All these small transactions can have a big impact, according to a report by Bosun Adebaki (a Business Consultant at Blockchain at Berkeley).[11] In recent years, the modern-day microfinance institutions Adebaki

---

[7]"Is the Overseas Money Transfer Industry Experiencing a Blockchain Effect?" https://www.cryptocurrency10.com/en/blog/cryptocurrencies/the-blockchain-effect-on-overseas-money-transfer-industry.

[8]More information about Stellar is available at https://www.stellar.org/.

[9]M.J. Casey and P. Vigna. 2014. "Mt. Gox, Ripple Founder Unveils Stellar, a New Digital Currency Project." https://blogs.wsj.com/moneybeat/2014/07/31/mt-gox-ripple-founder-unveils-stellar-a-new-digital-currency-project/.

[10]J. Bright. 2017. "Africa's SureRemit Joins the Tokenized Race to Win the Global Remittance Market," *TechCrunch*. https://techcrunch.com/2017/12/11/africas-sureremit-joins-the-tokenized-race-to-win-the-global-remittance-market/, (accessed August 28, 2018).

[11]B. Adebaki. 2019. "Microfinance and Alternative Data Meets the World of Blockchain." https://medium.com/blockchain-at-berkeley/microfinance-and-alternative-data-meets-the-world-of-blockchain-9aa7f8e39239.

The small transactions can have a big wing impact.

interviewed issued a combined $750 million in microloans to over 4.5 million customers in emerging economies across the globe.

Adebaki found that modern microfinance institutions can use mobile phone data to draw signals and inferences about behaviors that drive loan repayment. They have achieved, on average, repayment rates of over 90 percent, and their loan acceptance rates of 50 percent are significantly higher than those of traditional financial institutions. With loan decisions made in mere minutes, modern-day microfinance institutions are using algorithmic data-driven approaches as a catalyst for greater financial inclusion. They are allowing millions of underbanked individuals to grow their businesses or smoothen their income streams.[12]

Microfinance and Microlending on Blockchain Are a Real Opportunity

According to Adebaki, blockchain technology has the potential to foster significant growth in microfinance and provide effective solutions to

---

[12]Ibid.

potential obstacles. It can help verify a borrower's identity, create shared and trusted credit histories, enable more secure sharing and maintenance of sensitive data, and allow for a cheaper and quicker flow of capital to and from borrowers. According to Adebaki, blockchain technology faces adoption challenges, such as legacy contracts and infrastructure, as well as uncertainty in the early stage of the technology's regulatory scheme, particularly related to data.[13]

For example, BRAVO, an application for microtransactions powered by blockchain, uses cryptocurrencies to provide anonymous payments.[14] Maria Luna, CEO at BRAVO, explains,

> The cryptocurrency market is worth over $290 billion, but many users don't know how to acquire coins let alone where to spend them. Even though there is a strong and real case for service professionals, artists, small merchants, and everybody else to use it, for now, many shops and service professionals don't have the ability or a simple solution to accept cryptocurrency. BRAVO will change this and let anyone pay or get paid in cryptocurrency seamlessly—just like we do for fiat currency transactions. [15]

Uulala, a cost-effective financial services platform powered by blockchain technology, is facilitating and accelerating the financial inclusion of the under and unbanked.[16] It was designed to bring back microcredit and take advantage of blockchain technology to increase transparency and lower interest rates. The platform's decentralized nature eliminates the need for middlemen or central authorities. Further, smart contracts streamline the repayment of loans. The company is focused on enabling millions of unbanked and underbanked Latinos to complete commercial transactions that would otherwise be inaccessible or unaffordable.[17]

---

[13]Ibid.
[14]Sergeenkov. "How Blockchain Is Changing Money Transfers."
[15]Ibid.
[16]More information about Uulala is available at https://uulala.io/.
[17]M. Loughran. 2018. "The Power of Blockchain for Microfinance." https://medium.com/uulala/the-power-of-blockchain-for-microfinance-139c4e7029af.

There are numerous other examples of blockchain, when used in microfinance and microlending, solving long-standing challenges. For example, BanQu, the first blockchain economic identity technology to create economic opportunities for people around the world living in extreme poverty, uses a proprietary method to create a mashup of selfie-plus-iris scan for people with no access to technology or banking. It is then augmented by critical information, such as land rights, voter registration, relationship-based credit profiles, health records, or the like. BanQu is focused on providing solutions around the refugee crisis, food, medical care, payroll distribution in conflict zones, and increasing revenue streams for social enterprises via diaspora capital participation.[18]

In the end, blockchain can amplify and improve microfinance and microlending to help micro, small, and medium enterprises and individuals who are excluded because they do not meet rigid banking criteria or because the fees are too high. However, transactions do not need to be financial to take advantage of the microvalue and microtransactions features of blockchain. Microvalues and microtransactions have a far-reaching impact. Payments and banking are just the beginning. The power of small is increasingly visible in transportation, art, insurance, content creation, and several other fields.

Micropayments to Help Cars Communicate

Not so long ago, when we talked about communication, we meant human interactions. At the very least, we were referring to living creatures, not objects. Yet in the world of connected devices, our objects have friendships with other objects and people. They communicate. Increasingly, technologists are asking themselves how to improve communications between objects? How can they communicate better with *us*? And, of course, the most important question: how high will the cost of therapy be for all these objects who are not heard and feel misunderstood?! And yes the last question is a joke in case you are a reader that takes everything literally!

---

[18]More information about BanQu is available at https://banqu.co/.

How high will the cost of therapy should be for all connected objects that are not heard and feel misunderstood?!

Oaken Innovations[19] is a company that improves communication between cars and, in the process, works to solve important problems such as road congestion. Using micropayments, Oaken is building a decentralized platform for cars to negotiate the distance between each other and decrease urban congestion.

First, Oaken developed a blockchain-powered automated toll road system with connected cars. The solution eliminates the need for payment processors and expensive cloud infrastructure by using blockchain-powered IoT applications to automate toll road payments from vehicles. The project won them top honors in the entire world at the "UAE International Blockchain Hackathon."[20]

---

[19]More information about Oaken Innovations is available at https://www.oakeninnovations.com/.

[20]R. Ahmed. 208. "Oaken Innovations: The Blockchain Powered Vehicle Future." https://blog.bankofhodlers.com/oaken-innovations-the-blockchain-powered-vehicle-future/. See also https://www.oakeninnovations.com, https://devpost.com/software/project-vento.

Then, in early 2017, Oaken debuted its proof-of-concept, titled *Blockchain-Enabled Peer-to-Peer Car Links Application at Consensus* in New York. This application allows consumers to lease a vehicle from a car owner using a smart contract on the Ethereum blockchain. Combined with other technologies, the application allows you to lease and control access to the vehicle. The platform provides a ubiquitous data store for mobility capacity (cars available for hire) across all producers without the need for intermediaries like Uber and Lyft.[21]

Connected cars and sensors already communicate with each other. What they do not have is money for conducting transactions and paying for services that they provide to each other. In other words, their communication lacks a financial component.

Micropayments give cars an incentive to share data. For example, they can share information about a pothole, road congestion, or debris on the road. With payments or any exchange of value, the communication between cars and other objects becomes much more interesting and meaningful.

Just like it is more fun to earn real money that you can spend on products and services, rather than, say, Monopoly money that has no real value outside the game, cars that can exchange value, and not just communicate, can solve real problems and contribute more meaningfully. Through microvalues, we can incentivize drivers to avoid certain roads during peak rush hours, take alternative routes, report debris and potholes, map out new roads, and much, much more.

The value of small is not limited to money! Anything, especially of value, can be partitioned. In the process, the object gains new properties. This unlocks new ways to manage traditional assets.

Improving Content Creation and Distribution with Micropayments

In the end, micropayments are not a new concept. But blockchain may make them more practical. In fact, micropayments powered by blockchain may lead to entirely different business models. For example, blockchain provides for very low-priced content purchases, such as paying for

---

[21]Ibid.

Little acorns add up to a big stash.

reading a single news article, streaming a single song, or purchasing a clip art or image, at near-zero transaction costs. With a small fee, you may be able to transition from ad-sponsored content to ad-free alternatives for a small fee. With more accurate copyright tracking, cutting out various intermediaries, and additional layers of security, blockchain may allow consumers and users to pay a few cents for premium content rather than a blanket monthly subscription fee.[22]

For example, Kodak's KODAKOne, which tracks in a digital ledger who owns the rights to various images, provides photographers greater control over their work. The goal is for creators to automatically and quickly receive payments for content usage and combat pervasive content piracy problems.[23]

---

[22]T. Jenks. 2018. "Five Ways Blockchain Could Disrupt the Media Industry." https://www.verypossible.com/blog/five-ways-blockchain-could-disrupt-the-media-industry.
[23]C.R. Harvey, C. Moorman and M. Toledo. 2018. "How Blockchain Can Help Marketers Build Better Relationships with Their Customers." https://hbr.org/2018/10/how-blockchain-can-help-marketers-build-better-relationships-with-their-customers.

Fractional Ownership: A Masterpiece and Prime Real Estate within Your Reach

While you may not be able to afford the entire field, you may buy a flower.

A Piece of History or Masterpiece

Have you ever imagined climbing your grandmother's attic on a lazy Sunday afternoon and stumbling on a copy of the first print of the U.S. Constitution or a long-lost original Van Gogh? In my case, this dream had no chance of being a reality. All my grandparents live in an apartment complex with no access to the attic. And my family has moved around so much that, to the extent there has ever been anything of value or historical significance, it has already been discovered and sold by others a long time ago. And that is how I gave up all hope to ever own the first print of the U.S. Constitution or a lost original Van Gogh.

Eve Sussman is one of the artists at Snark.art,[24] a Brooklyn laboratory for art and technology that explores the ways blockchain can unleash creativity in art. One day, Eve, who works with film, video, and installation,

---

[24]More information about Snark.art is available at https://snark.art/.

wondered what happens when many people own a piece of a work of art. She shot a video piece called *89 Seconds at Alcázar*, recreating the famous Las Meninas 1656 painting by Diego Velázqueis, a masterpiece that now hangs at the Museo del Prado in Madrid.

Then she divided her original Ethereum-based video into 2,304 unique squares to create a new artwork on blockchain. She allowed collectors to purchase individual, unique blocks. The *89 Seconds at Alcázar* is in the collections of the Whitney Museum, the Museum of Modern Art, and Seoul's Leeum Samsung Museum, among others. As the white paper puts it, "The resulting blockchain-based artwork, 89 seconds Atomized, can be collected by a group of new owners, who are empowered to reassemble the full video at will." Eve's experiment is an example of fractional ownership, an intriguing concept enabled by blockchain that will challenge many of our existing models of ownership and assets.

Each square is registered on the Ethereum blockchain as a digital token ("atom"). It cannot be duplicated but can be freely traded or sold. It is offered at random for the price of $120. The purchaser receives an atom on the Ethereum blockchain (ERC-721). Each atom contains a full 10-minute 20×20 pixel video that can be viewed at Snark.art and stored in a digital wallet. Collectors can loan out atoms, or request a loan from the community, for public and private screenings. Individual atoms can also be bought or sold by collectors, and each is a piece of art on its own.

This approach allowed many people to own a part of Eve's work. It is also becoming a social experiment in ownership and collective interaction. Eve's work of art can be reassembled and screened at will by the community of collectors. So, what happens if some of the purchases don't want to display their unique block or somehow missed the notice to do so?

At this time, the unique blocks that do not have permission are not displayed and instead a black square appears. This obviously pushes the boundaries of what it means to own something collectively. What impact should each owner have on how the work is displayed? Should she be able to choose *not* to display it? Is being able to make that choice part of the dynamic nature of the artwork? Is the ability to experience the same artwork differently every time a central part of blockchain art experience?

Furthermore, Eve's artwork demonstrates that it is possible to create a unique digital artwork that has digital scarcity attributes. And in the process, she brings us much closer to the possibility of owning the first print of the U.S. Constitution or that long-lost original Van Gugh, one pixel at the time.

A Prime Location Real Estate Is within Your Reach, At Least in Part

Likewise, blockchain-based smart contract tokenization in real estate allows to create partial, or "fractionalized," unique digital ownership interests in real estate. Specifically, real estate owners can issue such fractionalized tokens to investors, disburse profits proportionally to each token holder, and empower token holders with voting power in the company's decision-making.

This allows token owners to trade tokens in secondary markets, which significantly increases liquidity within the real estate asset class. Of course, this method of ownership is novel and will likely be a turbulent one for a while. For years to come, numerous legal and business minds will develop new concepts and frameworks around fractional ownership.

Microinsurance: Ensuring Small Risks Is Big

The butterfly effect can be scaled across different industries.

When you were growing up, if your mother was anything like my mother, she probably told you not to talk to strangers and most definitely not to get into strangers' cars. Times have changed. Today you probably regularly talk to strangers online, use Uber and Lyft to ride with strangers, and through Airbnb live in strangers' houses and apartments. So it only makes sense that you rely on strangers to mitigate risks in your life.

Insuring Low-Income and Traditionally Excluded

Enter the world of microinsurance, which is not a new concept and has many meanings. One meaning of microinsurance is in protecting low-income people against disasters in exchange for a premium proportionate to the likelihood and cost of the risks. It is like regular insurance, but with a focus on low-income people or people who are ignored by mainstream insurance. It can be delivered in many ways, including small community-based schemes, various traditional microfinance institutions such as credit unions, and others. Blockchain provides a solution for this as well.

Surety.ai[25] is using blockchain and artificial intelligence back-end to ensure maximum security and privacy and to offer microinsurance to the unbanked in Asia. Through chatbot, social, mobile, and web, it allows insurers and financial advisers to connect effectively with customers and provide health, accident, property, and agriculture microinsurance.[26] Similarly, Hearti[27] allows insurance companies to connect with their customers by offering microinsurance, on-demand, and at affordable prices in Asia.

---

[25]For more information about Surety.ai is available at https://hearti.io/.

[26]K. Lim. 2019. "Microinsurance Is Key to Southeast Asian financial Inclusion." https://e27.co/microinsurance-is-key-to-southeast-asian-financial-inclusion-20190204/.

[27]More information about Hearti is available at https://hearti.io/.

Peer-to-Peer Transforms Microinsurance Further

Other companies are combining blockchain microinsurance capabilities with blockchain peer-to-peer capabilities. Nexus Mutual,[28] built on the Ethereum blockchain and using Ethereum smart contracts,[29] helps people spread risk across larger communities. It allows people from all over the world to share insurance risk, thus actually eliminating the need for an insurance company.

Nexus Mutual's goal is to lower insurance costs and replace the need for more established insurance companies. As Hugh Karp, the founder of Nexus Mutual, explained in one of the interviews,

> Our primary use of blockchain is to ensure the common pool of funds is not controlled by any one individual. It is held in smart contracts instead, which means funds can only be used under certain conditions.[30]

Others, such as iXLedger, the technology development arm of iX Technology Group,[31] and Teambrella[32] use blockchain to remove intermediaries, decrease costs, and shift to a peer-to-peer model.

Conclusion

As we've seen, blockchain's ability to harness the power of small is one of its greatest assets. By making quick, small sum payments easy and efficient, blockchain unlocks a world of possibilities for all industries. From the world of microinsurance to object-to-object communication, micropayments promise to smoothen out inefficiencies by eliminating unnecessary payments—and possibly even the roads we drive on by spreading

---

[28]More information about Nexus Mutual is available at https://www.nexusmutual.io/.

[29]https://github.com/somish/NexusMutual.

[30]E. Picco. 2019. "Blockchain in Insurance Use Case #5: Nexus Mutual." https://www.disruptordaily.com/blockchain-insurance-use-case-nexus-mutual/.

[31]More information about iXLedger is available at https://ixtechnology.com/ixledger/.

[32]More information about Teambrella is available at https://cryptoslate.com/coins/teambrella/.

information about potholes. Miscommunication and risk are inherent to life; but with blockchain, they'll become a lot less costly as usage-based or outcome-based business models evolve, assets are optimized, and products become more like services.

DADA Collective: Boris Toledo, Chile / Daveed, USA, collaboratively created using blockchain technology, a visual conversation.

Conclusion

DADA Collective: Simon Wairiuko, Kenya / Serste, Italy / Boris Toledo Doorm, Chile, collaboratively created using blockchain technology, a visual conversation.

Future of Blockchain

"What is the future of blockchain?" It's a question that comes up frequently when I speak to professionals of all backgrounds. There's obviously no right answer ... yet. With a technology that is innovating so rapidly and constantly evolving, there's no way to know what's in store.

Adoption Is Needed

According to Gartner, a leading business analyst, blockchain has been a highly searched term on its platform. Yet, its recent survey revealed that the current number of actual blockchain deployments in enterprises is scarce. Only 1 percent of CIOs indicated blockchain adoption within their organization, and only 8 percent were engaged in short-term planning or active experimentation with it. Furthermore, 77 percent said they had no plans to investigate it further.

So, it seems, people are curious, but not enough to embrace the technology. Based on this environment, some think that interest may be too low to justify significant blockchain investment now.[1]

---

[1] R. van der Meulen. 2017. "A Snapshot of an Emerging Blockchain Services Market." https://www.gartner.com/smarterwithgartner/a-snapshot-of-an-emerging-blockchain-services-market/.

Nonetheless, Gartner predicts that by 2025, the business value added by blockchain will grow to slightly over $176 billion. Although that in and of itself is a huge number, it predicts an enormous surge in the following few years to more than $3.1 trillion by 2030.

To ensure wide adoption of blockchain, businesses need to be clear about how they can make it profitable. Specifically, they need to articulate on two aspects: one, the value that blockchain brings that existing solutions do not; and two, how to capture this value through a profitable and sustainable business model.[2]

Blockchain Patent Filing Trends

Another way to predict the future of a technology is by reviewing patent filing trends. It's like an ultrasound during pregnancy: you can get a glimpse of what's developing before it's out there. Here are six trends in patent filings that Marc Kaufman, a Partner at Rimon Law, thinks might illuminate the path ahead for blockchain.[3]

Blockchain patents are increasingly common. Among those adopting the technology, many believe that, for various reasons, they will be generally immune to patent risks with the technology. Kaufman cautions that that assumption is wrong and that working with blockchain technology could be like walking through a minefield of patents. According to him, "A lot of parties are filing a lot of patent applications to cover a lot of aspects of blockchain technology."

There has been an exponential growth of blockchain-related patents. "Some parties, especially early on, purposely did not seek patents," Kaufman explains.

> For example, Satoshi, whoever this person is, never patented Bitcoin. Beginning around 2013 or 2014, when the technology really started to explode, this started to change. At first, we started to see a small number of filings. But since then, the increase in the numbers of patent publications worldwide has really taken off. In 2018, we saw over 2800 new patent families published worldwide. According

---

[2]M. Helfman. 2019. "Why Businesses Aren't Adopting Blockchain." https://medium .com/altcoin-magazine/why-businesses-arent-adopting-blockchain-1ee9c7af7cda.
[3]M. Kaufman. Discussions with the author. 2019.

to a conservative prediction, we will see 4,600 new patent families related to blockchain technology published in 2019. We have observed almost exponential growth in blockchain patent filings since 2013. I don't see a reason why it would slow down any time soon.

Patent families by 1st publication year

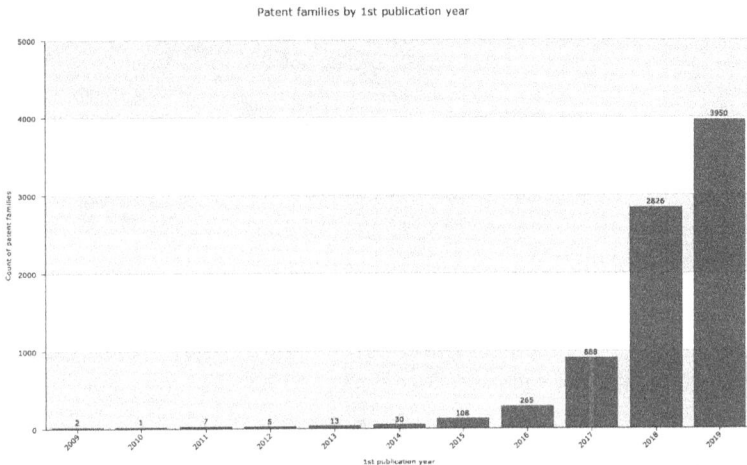

Based on a study prepared by Marc Kaufman. The number of published patent families per year since 2009, up through September of 2019.

The United States and China are leading the blockchain patent filing trend. "We're seeing blockchain patent applications in all the major markets of the world, but especially in the United States and China. We're also seeing more and more patents filed in Australia, some European countries, India, Brazil, and a few others," Kaufman explains. "Companies are most interested in filing where they think there will be a large market and/or they will find a friendly, or at least predictable, regulatory framework because they think their competitors will set up shop there soon."

According to Kaufman,

You see patent filings and corresponding registrations in Switzerland, Malta, Hong Kong, Japan, Singapore, and the Cayman Islands. We have already seen compelling commercial applications. It just makes sense to protect the revenue. It's the same cycle we saw with many other technologies, such as web technology, mobile networking, and semiconductors. It'll likely be a 5 to 15-year hockey stick kind of rise in patent filings. We're only seeing the beginning of this trend.

Patent families by Protection country

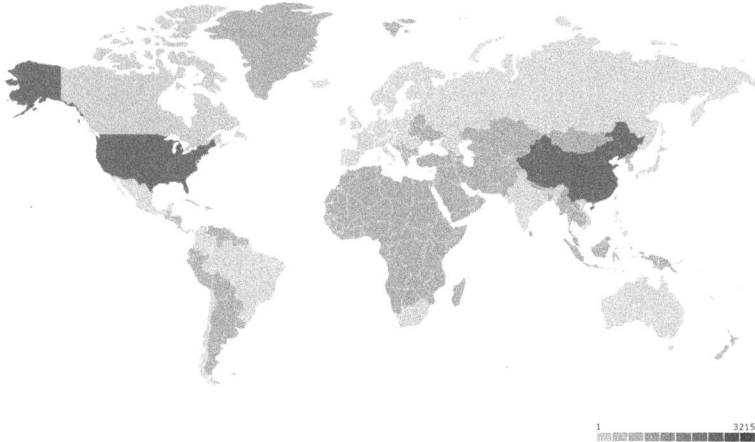

Based on a study prepared by Marc Kaufman. A map of where patent families are being originally filed. Darker blue means more patent publications.

Blockchain seems to attract unlikely competitors from different industries. "We see filings for blockchain patents from IBM, Accenture, Bank of America, Walmart, Alibaba, Microsoft, Mastercard, and several FinTech companies," Kaufman observes. These companies are not traditionally competing in the same industry. Where else would you see all these companies listed next to each other? Kaufman predicts that this trend of new competitors emerging may continue.

Patent families by Assignees

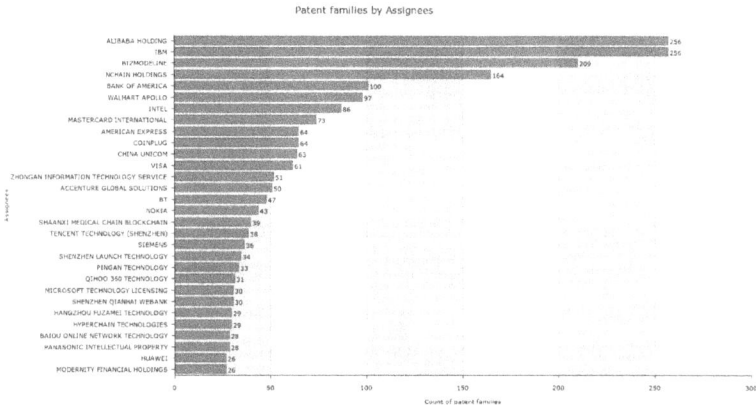

Based on a study prepared by Marc Kaufman. The blockchain patent owners and the number of published patent families owned by each.

Three years ago, the top 20 patent filers were dominated by research and academic institutions. Now the top 20 are mostly commercial institutions. Kaufman says, "We'll likely see more patents coming from companies for the purpose of making a profit." This is a clear indicator that blockchain technology is becoming widely perceived as commercially valuable and potentially profitable. He explains,

> For most technologies, you see universities and other research institutions doing most of the development in early stages. This was certainly true for the Internet. But as technologies are developed, companies increasingly file patent applications as part of their commercialization efforts. It seems that is where blockchain technology is now and will be for the foreseeable future.

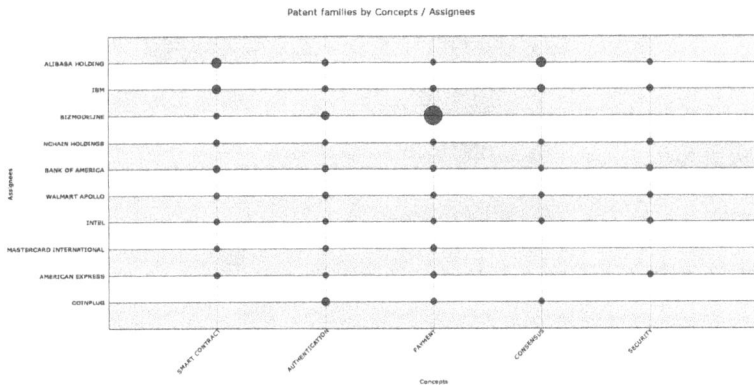

Based on a study prepared by Marc Kaufman. The blockchain patent owners plotted against the top technology categories. The larger the dot, the more patents in that category.

The top focus areas for current patent filings are authentication, payments, security, consensus, and smart contracts. The top filers tend to file across most, if not all, of these categories.

> We see a lot of patent filings in authentication, payments, security, consensus mechanisms, and smart contracts. We've seen a lot of filings related to authentication, payments, and security in the past 5 years. The others—around consensus and smart contracts—are more recent,

Kaufman observes. Companies tend to patent across a broad spectrum of technologies. It's typical of an early-stage technology when innovations occur across a broad spectrum of aspects of and uses for that technology.

The Crystal Ball Moment: Blockchain Is Here to Stay

Blockchain is here to stay!

As the examples in this book demonstrate, many different industries are being transformed by blockchain as you are reading this. To name a few, finance and banking, hedge funds, voting, advertising, education, Internet of Things (IoT), sports, charity, gaming, agriculture, gambling, law enforcement, publishing, real estate, identity, energy, insurance, music, supply chain, government, health care, pharmaceuticals, and others are all experimenting with blockchain technology and testing how it can strengthen their mission or their bottom line.[4]

---

[4]"Banking Is Only the Beginning: 55 Big Industries Blockchain Could Transform." 2019. https://www.cbinsights.com/research/industries-disrupted-blockchain/. See also B. Marr. 2018. "Here Are 10 Industries Blockchain Is Likely to Disrupt." https://www.forbes.com/sites/bernardmarr/2018/07/16/here-are-10-industries-blockchain-is-likely-to-disrupt/#454a6446b5a2; J. White. 2018. "9 Industries That Will Soon Be Disrupted by Blockchain." https://www.inc.com/john-white/9-industries-that-will-soon-be-disrupted-by-blockchain.html.

Across sectors, we are all learning together what is possible with this new, exciting tool.

However, there remains a question about blockchain platforms. Specifically, which one will emerge as the leading option? Will it be Hyperledger, Ethereum, or a third one—it's possible that it hasn't even been developed yet?

Of course, the underlying assumption of this question is that there will be one universal platform on top of which all users build. This convergence has been the story of the growth of the Internet—the platform on which all apps and services are built—and in some ways, the story of the modern technology boom more generally.

But what if blockchain develops more like an archipelago and less like an island—with multiple blockchains for different purposes? Each industry, project, and goal could have its own platform. Then you have a real choice in deciding where to build your apps. But importantly, interoperability and connectedness of these blockchain islands will become critical and a paramount obstacle that will have to be overcome.

It is increasingly apparent that blockchain is a very powerful tool. But that's exactly what it is: a tool. It is not a discipline nor is it a product. In other words, there will be no blockchain majors emerging from major STEM institutions. The classic disciplines, law, engineering, medicine, and economics, are here to stay. The major industries, music, health care, and real estate, are also here to stay. These disciplines and industries will be heavily influenced by blockchain and vice versa—but they will work in concert and will not be replaced.

A Sea of Challenges (aka, an Amazing Opportunity for Some Very Brave Souls)

At this stage, to say that blockchain has challenges is an understatement. The difficulties ahead should not be overlooked or discounted.

Growing Pains Are Real

First, it is still early, very early. As a high schooler in 1995, I heard the word "web" for the first time, but no one could explain to me what it was, much less how it would transform my life and become essential to nearly every aspect of being alive. But by the year 2000, when the Internet was emerging as the hottest trend and I was a college student in search of a distraction, I took a few minutes to download funny cat pictures at the UC Berkeley library. And now, just 15 years later, my life would most definitely be incomplete—and likely impossible—without the Internet. In fact, I get frustrated when my video streaming slows down for a few seconds under the Bay Bridge when I take the train to San Francisco every morning.

Like me in 1995, though many people have heard of blockchain and read an article or two on it, most still can't really understand what it is or how their life will be incomplete without it. While the innovation is happening at a breakneck pace, the benefits of this complex technology are still a bit too abstract and removed from the average pedestrian. In sum, these are still early days. You are not late in the game. In fact, right now is the perfect time to get involved.

Blockchain Is a Very Complex Technology

Second, this technology is technically complicated. If you google "what is blockchain," you will find a sea of videos and articles that discuss ledgers, cryptology, decentralization, smart contracts, and many other abstract concepts that you have never heard before. And it might take some time for you to grasp it.

But there's good news! Like any technology we use every day, you don't have to understand the technical details underlying blockchain to appreciate the many applications and benefits of blockchain. Just like we enjoy the benefits of electricity without understanding basic physics and discussing electrons, it is possible to enjoy the benefits of blockchain without knowing cryptology or getting into the weeds on ledgers.

Blockchain Rollercoaster: From FOMO to FUD

Third, the price and hype fluctuations in blockchain are overwhelming and intimidate most normal people. The rollercoaster ride between "fear of missing out" (FOMO) and "fear, uncertainty, and doubt" (FUD) is just not everyone's cup of tea. For example, in 2017, we saw a coin go up to $20,000! Now, what is it today? A fraction of that. The hype cycle in blockchain is not for the faint of heart and we will likely have at least a few more soon. Yet, the most powerful companies of tomorrow are being built today. That's why the time to be involved is now.

Regulators by the Dozen and More

Fourth, the regulatory challenges are as complex as the technology itself. Everybody from the SEC to the IRS has an opinion on blockchain and wants to regulate it according to its own ideas. The challenge is that most of the regulators do not understand this technology and cannot keep up with its developments. As part of my job, I have spoken with many legislators and regulators at the state and federal levels and, from those conversations, have drawn two conclusions. One, it may take a while for regulators to achieve comfort and clarity and for us to trade digital assets freely. And two, there will be a web of multiple regulators and legislations for anything blockchain-related.

The Missing Code of Ethics

Fifth, questionable ethics and plain illegal behavior are abundant in the blockchain industry, though thankfully both are diminishing. Fraud has been abundant. There's no Federal Deposit Insurance Corporation (FDIC). The persistent story over the last few years is Bitcoin being used for illegal or illicit activities, or millions of dollars evaporating somehow that even the forensic accounts can't trace. This is a huge downside for most people!

Many scholars and other professionals have proposed ethical frameworks for blockchain. For example, Cara LaPointe proposed The Blockchain Ethical Design Framework for Social Impact to "ensure that social value is protected."[5]

---

[5]More information, C. LaPointe. 2018. "The Blockchain Ethical Design Framework for Social Impact." https://beeckcenter.georgetown.edu/blockchain-ethical-design-framework-social-impact/.

Chelsea Rustrum,[6] who originally wrote a book about the sharing economy (shareablelife.com) and developed theories around collaboration, travel, and entrepreneurship, got involved with blockchain early. She is another person who feels that we need to be more conscious of ethics when working with blockchain. She evolved from prioritizing access over ownership to the need for shared ownership and value distribution among all value creators in business.

> She also saw that blockchain technology has the potential to be the connective layer between emergent technologies like IoT, virtual reality/augmented reality, sensors, artificial intelligence, and robotics. How we program our technologies will have far-reaching implications for all stakeholders of computing, which is every person on this planet. The technologies that run our world must be programmed with the humanistic and ecological values we want to see now and in the future, so thoughtful dialogue, consideration, and debate need to happen in these areas. Blockchain for Good is leading this charge.

Rustrum came up with the Blockchain Code of Ethics[7] for blockchain. She explains,

> I've been working on the Blockchain Code of Ethics for about a year now, maybe a little bit longer. I started with a 60-page research document, and then created a series of ethics and ethical areas, subject areas you could say. There are now 12 subject areas and 50 ethics that have been prewritten to be discussed. They came from all kinds of sources. They are now in the Liquid Democracy platform for discussion and comments.

There are, of course, numerous other concerns with blockchain. Security, privacy, poor design, scalability, and interoperability are just a few other visible challenges.

---

[6]C. Rustrum. Discussions with the author. 2019.

[7]More information about the Blockchain Code of Ethics is available at http://blockchaincodeofethics.com/.

WE THE PEOPLE, THE CREATORS, DEVELOPERS,
THE BUSINESS LEADERS, CULTURE DESIGNERS OF OUR TIME, ENDEAVOR
TO CREATE A FRAMEWORK FOR ETHICAL BLOCKCHAIN
COMPANIES, WHICH WILL HOLD ORGANIZATIONS ACCOUNTABLE TO:

HUMANITY	DATA	STAKEHOLDERS	VALUE CREATORS
THE PLANET	THE ECONOMY	DIVERSITY	TRANSPARENCY
FREEDOM	FUTURE TECHNOLOGIES	COMMUNITY	INTEGRITY

THIS IS OUR DECREE: We're committed to a decentralized future, focused on **humans first, protecting the planet always.**
We believe that all humans are stakeholders of **computing.** ALL. WE THE PEOPLE,
USE OUR MIND AND CONSCIENCE TO COLLECTIVELY CO-CREATE A VISION
FOR OUR VALUES, WHICH WE ACTIVATE WITH AND THROUGH TECHNOLOGY.
WE BELIEVE in peer-to-peer digital currencies, backed by real value—and incentivizing human behaviors **to improve all life.**
We believe in global equity and borderless commerce.
We build because **we must**—for the sake of global CONNECTIVITY,
FREEDOM, AND THE DESIRE TO CREATE UNCONVENTIONAL SOLUTIONS.
WE HAVE THE RESPONSIBILITY TO INCLUDE ALL THOSE IMPACTED BY
THE DECISIONS TECHNOLOGY MAKES—TO EDUCATE, INVITE, AND REACH OUT TO ALL STAKEHOLDERS
OF OUR CREATIONS. We know diversity is the key to interdependent commerce and build onramps of inclusion in every aspect of our **respective businesses.**
We think of our data like our digital doubles, **protecting and valuing individuals rights** to their OWN FOOTPRINT.
WE ENDEAVOR TO SHARE VALUE WITH THOSE WHO CREATE VALUE,
VALUE, WHEN AND WHERE VALUE IS CREATED.
WE BELIEVE in integrity, truthful statements, clear communication, and ownership of missteps, and the importance of accurate, **timely information.**
We're creating real value. Our tokens, coins, and currencies are backed by something greater than hype. **We program our values into our code** with future technologies IN MIND.
AND WE WILL CONTINUE TO REVISE OUR DECREE AS WE LEARN AND GROW.

BLOCKCHAIN FOR GOOD

Blockchain Code of Ethics Manifesto.

What Is Your Blockchain Strategy? Bridging Blockchain Vision and Reality

In 2018 PwC surveyed 600 executives and concluded:

- 84 percent of respondents are actively involved with blockchain
- 45 percent believe trust could delay adoption
- 28 percent believe interoperability of systems is a key to success.[8]

---

[8]PWC. "Blockchain Is Here. What's Your Next Move?" https://www.pwc.com/gx/en/issues/blockchain/blockchain-in-business.html.

Moreover, a Deloitte survey concluded that, "The only real mistake we believe organizations can make regarding blockchain right now is to do nothing."[9]

All this talk about blockchain possibilities is very intriguing and exciting. But for now it's just talk; how do we make it real? How do we build useful blockchain applications?

Problems Lead Innovation for Your Customers

All innovation, including blockchain, must be designed to solve problems. People do not need to know your approach. Customers have many needs—functionality, price, efficiency, transparency, convenience, compatibility, experience, design, reliability performance, control, options, information, accessibility, and numerous others[10]—that need to be addressed. At the end of the day, the customer is buying a solution, not a technology. That is why all successful companies start with the problem. Do not start with a blockchain solution and then look for a problem. Blockchain may or may not solve the problem you identify.

In fact, you may need to combine blockchain with other technologies, systems, and processes to solve the problem you first identified. Remember blockchain is a back-end technology. When it works, you can't see it. Relatedly, blockchain becomes even more interesting when it's combined with other technologies, such as artificial intelligence, good data, and IoT. It meshes well with existing technologies, like smartphones. So the solution to the problem you are trying to solve will likely require a bouquet of technologies.

Lastly, understanding your customers and their pains is key. That is why it is so important that everyone on the team talk to customers. This way, great ideas can come from many people, not just a select few. Your entire team can drive innovation because different people can hear and interpret customer feedback differently.

---

[9]Deloitte. 2018. "2018 Global Blockchain Survey." https://www2.deloitte.com/content/dam/Deloitte/cz/Documents/financial-services/cz-2018-deloitte-global-blockchain-survey.pdf.

[10]A. Breschi. 2019. "16 Types of Customer Needs (and How to Solve for Them)." https://blog.hubspot.com/service/customer-needs.

Pilot and Collaborate to Learn

Then, pilot to learn. Remember: this technology is very complicated. There are very few experts, and certainly none with decades of experience. Everyone is learning together. And the only way to learn is by doing. That's why it's so important to experiment, pilot, and design proof of concepts. To learn and be a part of the conversation. That is how you stay in the game.

Though innovation sometimes comes from internal research and development efforts, large enterprises figure out other ways. A large company can partner, invest, or acquire, among many other options. A large enterprise may leverage its resources and network to learn in many ways.

The reason to do pilots internally is partially to develop and stabilize a great idea. You learn a lot in the process. For example, you can start to figure out how it applies in the context of your industry, your business, or the problems that your clients are trying to solve. If you're negotiating your next partnership or investment, you do not want to be the dumbest person at the table. That is why you learn from pilots and proof of concepts.

There are numerous incentives for enterprises and start-ups to collaborate. The former brings resources, experience, and industry connections. The latter brings risk-taking, creativity, cutting-edge technology, and speed of innovation. If done right, collaboration can bring a magnificent outcome.

Blockchain is inherently a team effort, with potentially huge benefits to those who achieve network effects. That's why we see so much collaboration in the industry. For example, Hyperledger has over 250 members.[11]

---

[11]M. Draper. 2018. "11 Blockchain Projects Flaunting High-Profile Partnerships & Collaborations." https://hackernoon.com/11-blockchain-projects-flaunting-high-profile-partnerships-collaborations-e41aeb410813. See also, B.M. Krishna. 2018. "Startup to Help Traditional Businesses Effectively Embrace Blockchain Technologies." https://cointelegraph.com/news/startup-to-help-traditional-businesses-effectively-embrace-blockchain-technologies; J. Miller. 2018. "Four Reasons Why Blockchain Startups and Corporates Should Collaborate." https://www.ibm.com/blogs/blockchain/2018/12/four-reasons-why-blockchain-startups-and-corporates-should-collaborate/.

Blockchain Is Custom, Not a Miracle Out-of-the-Box Solution

Though a lot of companies have misguided expectations that blockchain is an out-of-the-box miracle cure, it is still an emerging technology. We still have a very long way to go. Currently, the majority of blockchain solutions are custom, not standard. This means that they will take time and resources to be developed and implemented.

So why should you engage with blockchain now? Simple. If you don't get your hands dirty, you are missing out on learning. You won't know what this technology can do and what it means for your organization, both from a threat and an opportunity perspective. And yes, the easy-to-implement, budget-friendly, widely available, quality-proven, quick-to-deploy, no-technical-experience-required, out-of-the-box solutions are coming. We're just not there yet.

Learn from Prior Technologies

Learning doesn't have to come from experimenting with current blockchain technology alone. You can learn from past technologies, such as the Internet. Just like with the Internet's first 10 years, if you look at the blockchain landscape you'll notice that many companies are infrastructure-focused. We've been building mining companies, coins, exchanges, and protocols.

If you look back on the Internet, you'll notice that, after the first 10 years, we spent the next 10 to 20 years building companies like Facebook and Amazon—companies that are very different from what we saw in the first 10 years, such as Microsoft and AOL. Similarly, it is likely that in the next 10 to 20 years, we will be building products and services and not just infrastructure. And, in the books, you saw just a glimpse of what's to come.

Cultivate a Global Community of Loyal Users and Developers

Community is an important element of anything blockchain-related partially because network effects are very important for any project or application to succeed. It helps to convert casual followers into raving fanatics to propel your project forward. Community, however, is different from customers. Some community members can also be customers, though they don't have to be. Community members need to be recruited and onboarded carefully.

Uniting around a compelling purpose and mission is a great start. Creating persistent traditions and regular cadence may help to manage the community's expectations and baseline standards. For example, it is not unusual to have weekly, monthly, or quarterly ask-me-anything (AMA) virtual sessions on Twitter or Reddit. Creating a consistent community culture and using sophisticated tools are both essential.

Similarly, on the enterprise side of things, you have your consortium-based blockchain technology, which is really just another community. In a consortium-based model, a couple of members, typically including a founding member, ask other members to join. This model tends to be challenging because reaching consensus among different stakeholders who may even be competitors is never an easy task. Questions often arise, for example, who has permissions and access?, how to add new members?, how to remove a member violating agreements?, making things political.

There are many legal requirements that have nothing to do with technology. You must also show that there's value to pursuing this new model—answer the nagging question of "what's in it for me?"—which is not always easy.

Likewise, it is very important to create a broad developer community. It is hard, but crucial, to recruit the best technologists and developers available. You need to show the openness and usefulness of the technology you're building and then make it easy and enticing for developers to get engaged.

About the Author

Olga V. Mack is the CEO of Parley Pro, a next-generation contract management company that has pioneered online negotiation technology. Olga embraces legal innovation and had dedicated her career to improving and shaping the future of law. She is convinced that the legal profession will emerge even stronger, more resilient, and more inclusive than before by embracing technology. She shares her views in her columns on Above the Law, Bloomberg Law, Newsweek, and many other publications. Olga is also an award-winning general counsel, operations professional, start-up advisor, public speaker, adjunct professor, and entrepreneur. Olga authored *Get on Board: Earning Your Ticket to a Corporate Board Seat and Fundamentals of Smart Contract Security*.

Index

OTHER TITLES IN THE ENTREPRENEURSHIP AND SMALL BUSINESS MANAGEMENT COLLECTION

Scott Shane, Case Western University, *Editor*

- *Native American Entrepreneurs* by Ron F. Sheffield
- *Small Business Management: A Road Map for Survival During Crisis* by Andreas Karaoulanis
- *How to Succeed as a Solo Consultant: Breaking Out on Your Own* by Stephen D. Field
- *From Starting Small to Winning Big: The Definitive Digital Marketing Guide For Startup Entrepreneurs* by Shishir Mishra
- *Dynastic Planning: A 7-Step Approach to Family Business Succession Planning and Related Conflict Management* by Walid S. Chiniara
- *The Rainmaker: Start-Up to Conglomerate* by Jacques Magliolo
- *The Entrepreneurial Adventure: Embracing Risk, Change, and Uncertainty* by David James
- *On All Cylinders, Second Edition: Succeeding as an Entrepreneur and a Leader* by Ron Robinson
- *Cultivating an Entrepreneurial Mindset* by Tamiko L. Cuellar
- *From Vision to Decision: A Self-Coaching Guide to Starting a New Business* by Dana K. Dwyer
- *Get on Board: Earning Your Ticket to a Corporate Board Seat* by Olga V. Mack
- *Department of Startup: Why Every Fortune 500 Should Have One* by Ivan Yong Wei Kit
- *Family Business Governance: Increasing Business Effectiveness and Professionalism* by Keanon J. Alderson
- *Can You Run Your Business With Blood, Sweat, and Tears? Volume I* by Stephen Elkins-Jarrett
- *Can You Run Your Business With Blood, Sweat, and Tears? Volume II* by Stephen Elkins-Jarrett
- *Can You Run Your Business With Blood, Sweat, and Tears? Volume III* by Stephen Elkins-Jarrett
- *Getting to Market With Your MVP: How to Achieve Small Business and Entrepreneur Success* by J.C. Baker
- *The Leadership Development Journey: How Entrepreneurs Develop Leadership Through Their Lifetime* by Jen Vuhuong

Concise and Applied Business Books

The Collection listed above is one of 30 business subject collections that Business Expert Press has grown to make BEP a premiere publisher of print and digital books. Our concise and applied books are for…

- Professionals and Practitioners
- Faculty who adopt our books for courses
- Librarians who know that BEP's Digital Libraries are a unique way to offer students ebooks to download, not restricted with any digital rights management
- Executive Training Course Leaders
- Business Seminar Organizers

Business Expert Press books are for anyone who needs to dig deeper on business ideas, goals, and solutions to everyday problems. Whether one print book, one ebook, or buying a digital library of 110 ebooks, we remain the affordable and smart way to be business smart. For more information, please visit **www.businessexpertpress.com**, or contact **sales@businessexpertpress.com**.

www.ingramcontent.com/pod-product-compliance
Lightning Source LLC
Chambersburg PA
CBHW061156220326
41599CB00025B/4508